WORK
then
PLACE

Navigating Modern Work
and Where it Happens

WORK
then
PLACE

Sara Escobar | Corinne Murray

MUNN
AVENUE
PRESS

WORK Then PLACE
Navigating Modern Work
& Where it Happens
by Sara Escobar and Corinne Murray

First Edition
Copyright © 2025 by Sara Escobar and Corinne Murray

Published by
Munn Avenue Press
300 Main Street, Ste 21
Madison, NJ 07940
MunnAvenuePress.com

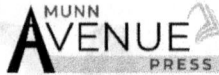

A MUNN
AVENUE
PRESS

For permission requests, contact MunnAvenuePress.com

Paperback ISBN: 978-1-960299-97-0
Hardcover ISBN: 978-1-960299-98-7
Printed in the United States of America

To our families, both given and chosen.

Contents

Contents

Contents

Contents

Introduction

We're on a mission to make work suck less.

We began writing the first version of this book in 2020, but then everything in our work and workplaces changed because of COVID-19. In an instant, the Great Work from Home (WFH) Experiment began, and corporate workers, many of whom had never worked from home before, were thrust into remote work. This seismic shift propelled a previously niche and nerdy conversation about the expansive future of work and all its opportunities into the foreground. Five years later, the proof is even clearer: This conversation should have been front and center all along.

Before the onset of COVID-19, experts projected that modifications to how and where work happens would evolve gradually, one change at a time. Instead, we find ourselves in a pressure cooker of change that extends far beyond how and where work should be done. The 2020s ushered in an era of labor awareness that hadn't existed in the United States since the 1960s. Knowledge workers—office workers defined by the mostly cognitive nature of their tasks and responsibilities—have historically benefited most from innovations and advancements in Workplace and Employee Experience. However, recent years have proven that, despite the prestige that knowledge work has always carried in society, this labor group is among the most vulnerable to current economic headwinds and the pendulum-swinging perspectives on modern work and its future trajectory.

In 2020, once knowledge workers had settled into the new rhythm of working from home, a more significant change began to take root. Working from home—just one of many distributed working modes in the modern era—offered knowledge workers a hint of alternate worklife realities, and many seized the opportunity to make different and, hopefully, better choices for themselves. Some moved to the cities they had always dreamed of living in. Others opted to move closer to family. Some chose digital nomadism, and some built families, businesses, and more. Regardless of the paths people found themselves on, the Great WFH Experiment inspired them to redesign their lives to achieve a better balance and ease, and prioritize the things that mattered to them. All the while, work carried on, albeit with a bit more existential dread than before.

Now, every teammate, regardless of their location, was just a direct message or video call away. It was a new, albeit often awkward, way to access one another. Without the office providing structure for work behaviors and organizational hierarchies, the fault lines in companies' operational and cultural foundations became increasingly visible to the average employee. Unfortunately, most companies weren't prepared or willing to reckon with the added scrutiny. Instead, they opted to wait till things got back to "normal," aligning with Goldman Sachs CEO David Solomon, who said, "[remote work is] an aberration that we are going to correct as soon as possible" *(Bloomberg 2021)*.

Companies like Amazon, AT&T, Boeing, Dell, J.P. Morgan, Nike, and *The Washington Post* have cited innovation, collaboration, and the broad desire to "rebuild" their cultures as the reasons behind bringing workers back to the office five days a week. That's because despite research revealing that over 80 percent of employees reported high productivity at home, more than half of managers believe the opposite *(Microsoft 2022)*. Companies introduced Return to Office mandates, many of which were stricter than pre-2020 in-office expectations, confirming research from Future Forum that showed 66 percent of executives developed post-COVID work plans with little input from employees *(Future Forum 2021)*.

Despite all this, Return to Office mandates have not succeeded in bringing people back to the office. Research from COVID-19 times indicates that, despite changes in company policies, flexible work behavior hasn't reversed. Instead, more than half of US workers now split their time between home and office, and 30 percent of remote-capable workers are in fully remote arrangements *(Deloitte 2023; Gallup 2023)*. In just a few short years, workplace flexibility—which was rarely considered an employee benefit until after 2020—is now second only to compensation when candidates are considering new roles *(Zoom 2023)*. Economist and Stanford professor Nick Bloom concluded that "since 2023, WFH and remote work behaviors have reached a point of normalization," and senior executives have even begun to concede the permanence of hybrid models and their likelihood of growth through 2028 *(Bloom, Han, and Liang 2024; McKinsey 2022)*.

Executives are not wrong for wanting thriving company cultures where community, collaboration, and innovation come easily. However, their misstep lies in the assumption that Return to Office mandates alone could ever yield these outcomes. That's because the overwhelming majority of Return to Office mandates are concerned with where people work, not how. But how people work and how organizations enable them is what is at the heart of companies' challenges.

The Age of AI and the Fourth Industrial Revolution are forcing leaders to confront a hard truth: Return to Office mandates barely scratch the surface of the transformation their organizations actually need. Focusing solely on where workers are located during work hours distracts from the more urgent task of building the structural and behavioral adaptability and agility needed to thrive in a volatile and fast-moving business environment.

Previous industrial revolutions—fueled by the introduction of steam, electricity, and early automation—set the stage for this fourth iteration, which began in earnest in the mid 2010s and has seen countless cross-industry disruptions brought on by AI *(McKinsey, 2022)*. Today, nearly 90 percent of executives say their business model is under more pressure than ever before as they navigate rapid, systemic change to their businesses and the broader market *(McKinsey 2023; Accenture 2025)*. In wake of the Great WFH Experiment, one certainty has emerged: workplace and operational transformation can't succeed without first reshaping and improving how people work, starting with their fundamental behaviors.

For many, this is a daunting task. Thoughts about cost, time, and effort are enough to bring momentum and enthusiasm to a grinding halt. However, it doesn't have to be this way, especially when we consider the organizational strengths that are built under these circumstances. It is no wonder then that companies with adaptive cultures can recover from disruption 2.6 times faster than those without and are five times more likely to have high-performing workforces *(McKinsey 2021; i4cp 2024).*

We created *WORK then PLACE* to help companies experiment with small, measurable changes that transform how work happens and to cultivate a resilient and agile workforce that is well-resourced and primed for navigating the business challenges of the twenty-first century.

The first step? To quote Arthur Ashe, the world-renowned twentieth-century tennis player and activist: "Start where you are."

Why We Wrote This Book

Until companies have a clear understanding of how work happens within their organization, along with its importance, what it entails, and whether it remains relevant in twenty-first-century work, they will miss out on the productivity, innovation, and opportunity gains that executives are seeking. *WORK then PLACE* offers a sequential process that guides companies through an experimentation and standardization process, marrying experimentation and continuous improvement with traditional organizational and workplace transformation methodologies.

The mission of *WORK then PLACE* is to help companies strengthen the dialogue between how work happens in their organizations and the broader trajectory of the business. The pace of change in the Fourth Industrial Revolution is not slowing down, and, unless companies act, the current frustrations and challenges will only be exacerbated. There is a Chinese proverb that says, "The best time to plant a tree is twenty years ago; the second best time is now." Making a change now is always better—and easier—than making a change later.

We want to help executives embrace this new era of movement and innovation with confidence. Transformation and change in business are often viewed as high-effort, high-risk endeavors, leading many to be wary of them. *WORK then PLACE* was designed to be a catalyst for change, without demanding massive, overnight shifts. With the help of case studies, practical frameworks, and implementation guidance that translates strategy into action, *WORK then PLACE* can be your guide to launching a new initiative or untangling a stuck one. The goal is to build organizational resilience and agility by making incremental changes to key aspects of work and business. As these outcomes coalesce and compound, a new company culture centered on productivity, collaboration, and innovation can emerge. Similar to self-help and personal development methodologies, *WORK then PLACE* guides companies to approach change with a 1 percent-better-everyday mentality that can yield powerful results with fewer risks.

This approach is supported by insights from both Boston

Consulting Group (BCG) and Deloitte. Small, consistent nudges, like revisiting and reorienting meeting norms, adjusting team rituals, and embedding distributed work agreements into workflows, build momentum and resilience over time, enabling compounding value that leads to major shifts. *(BCG 2023; Deloitte Insights 2023).*

Who *WORK then PLACE* is for

The *WORK then PLACE* method is intentionally sequential; by building behavioral clarity before making environmental changes, organizations create lasting transformation. We wrote this book for executives and operational leaders who are taking on the vast opportunities that modern work presents and are willing, if not eager, to navigate uncertainty with an experimental and innovative mindset. It is written from the perspective of the doers within your organization—the people who are building the offices, writing the policies, and creating the digital ecosystems—who are dedicated to designing and maintaining the best working conditions possible for your workforce and the greatest chance of success for your company.

For Executives and Senior Leaders

You may be focused on organizational strategy, business impact, and cross-functional alignment. Prioritize the introductions and conclusions of each phase to understand strategic intent and expected outcomes. Use the frameworks to guide your leadership teams, focusing especially on Catalyze and Evolve, which emphasize capability building and long-term resilience.

Tip: You don't need to read every tactical detail. Instead, look for language and structures you can use to align your leadership team around a shared vision of workplace effectiveness.

For HR, Real Estate, and IT Practitioners

If you're responsible for implementing change, the middle sections of each chapter offer tactical value—frameworks, real-world case examples, and sequencing guides. Use these chapters as a toolkit for planning, diagnosing, and course-correcting initiatives.

Tip: The Knowledge Base and Position chapters are foundational to understanding the material. They ensure your strategy is behaviorally grounded before space, policy, or tooling decisions are made.

For Change Agents, Consultants, or Advisers

You likely work across departments or clients and are accustomed to ambiguity. Focus on the connective tissue between the *WORK then PLACE* phases—the feedback loops, governance structures, and patterns of misalignment that derail transformation.

Tip: Treat it as a diagnostic map. Identify where a team is stuck, what steps they've skipped, or which systems (behavioral, cultural, digital) are under strain—then apply the right phase to unlock progress.

How to Use *WORK then PLACE*

WORK then PLACE is a play on the word "workplace," which is such an abstract concept that it holds different meanings for different industries and the people within them. The most common understanding is that "workplace" is synonymous with "office." This book aims to debunk this notion and broaden our collective knowledge of the workplace to accommodate the twenty-first-century realities of technology, cultural norms, and organizational structures that support flexible and distributed work.

Modern work demands that we have a deep understanding of how work gets done and the possibilities for evolution and innovation in the future before engaging in more traditional transformation processes. Return to Office mandates are hardly a drop in the bucket when discussing the future of work, especially when we realize how broad our task truly is. Section 1 of this book lays the foundation for the *WORK then PLACE* process by clarifying current terminology, identifying outdated concepts that need reimagining, and outlining the core concepts and fixtures required to embark on change successfully. Before we make changes to our reality, we need to understand how and why we got to where we are today.

We believe that the workplace is higher in the white-collar work hierarchy than the office, creating an undeniable alliance among operational teams, such as HR, Real Estate & Facilities, and IT. When these three cohorts work together toward the same objective of supporting employees as they generate high-quality work, the needs of the business and the desires of employees converge, creating progress for the company.

This reality is best achieved through behavioral experiments focused on productivity and effectiveness at the employee level, which create the groundswell for change across the organization. Within the pages of this book, you will find a guided process for behavior change around work, detailed in Section 2. Only after this momentum exists can companies successfully implement traditional forms of workplace and organizational transformation. Section 3 outlines these more familiar approaches that transform the structures of a workplace and an organization.

Just like the name letter poems your teachers might have had you write in elementary school (*C-harismatic, O-riginal, R-adical, I-ntutive, N-atural, N-eat, E-xuberant,* and *S-assy, A-ssertive, R-ealistic, A-mbitious, respectively*), we have structured this book by creating acronyms of the two pillars of this book: *WORK then PLACE.*

W-hat & Why	**P**-osition
O-perationalize	**L**-everage
R-egulate	**A**-dapt
K-nowledge	**C**-atalyze
	E-volve

WORK then PLACE does not offer instructions; it provides a navigation system that companies can use to chart their unique course. We believe in frameworks that create structure but are not so rigid that everyone achieves the same results. With *WORK then PLACE,* companies can experience the co-creative possibilities for executives, people managers, and individual contributors that help organizations and teams create practical and sustainable solutions, clearing the way for a better work reality.

The chapters that follow serve two purposes. First, they surface the complex dynamics shaping modern work and the workplaces that support it. Section 1 explores these foundational ideas, establishing the context for everything that follows.

Second, the book guides you through the full *WORK then PLACE* process, detailed in Sections 2 and 3. In the *WORK* phases, you'll define, operationalize, regulate, and scale the behaviors that make modern work effective within your organization. In the *PLACE* phases, you'll use those insights to shape your environment—positioning, leveraging, adapting, catalyzing, and evolving your physical, digital, and cultural systems.

Each chapter offers a combination of practical frameworks, real-world examples, and implementation guidance—designed to support both strategic planning and everyday decision-making. So, whether you're launching a transformation or refining one already in motion, this process gives you a structured path from friction to function, from reaction to intention.

You don't have to read this book cover to cover for it to be helpful. Feel free to start with the phase most relevant to your current challenge, just be sure the behavioral groundwork from the earlier stages is solidly in place. Each step builds on the one before it, and skipping ahead without that foundation can compromise the results you're working toward. We encourage you to use this book as a reference manual, rather than a one-time read. Return to the frameworks, stories, and phase guidance as your company's needs evolve.

Who We Are

We, the authors—Sara and Corinne—have built careers around work, the workplace, and the human experience. Academically, we have explored organizational psychology, change management, communications, and interdisciplinary studies with a focus on world cultures, religions, societal structures, and history. Professionally, we have over thirty years of combined experience working with major brands like American Express, CBRE, Hulu, Netflix, Riot Games, and WeWork.

We've designed new offices and created Employee Experience programs for global companies, developed and implemented organizational changes to how and where people work, and created methodologies to make these changes happen by launching these efforts to support upward of hundreds, sometimes thousands, of employees facing drastic changes to their day-to-day work. We've measured program and project success and worked to continuously improve the built environment, company culture, and Employee Experience, all of which contribute to overall company success.

Moreover, we have spent the past five years working with companies as they grapple with the most drastic changes to work that many of us have seen in our professional lives. We've learned what works and what doesn't, without losing momentum, and we've committed ourselves to continuous learning to understand the ongoing evolution of the workplace.

In short, we've lived at each stage of the workplace life cycle. *WORK then PLACE* came to be because we understand a workplace's inherent power and know what it looks like to have that power channeled to support collaboration, innovation, and community. When done well, the world of the workplace can be downright magical. However, workplace magic doesn't live in the walls of an office or the desks we sit at. What we've discovered is that the magic that executives crave relies heavily on how the companies they work for facilitate their ability to create high-quality work.

For modern work to be well supported by your company's workplace, it will require more than just talking points about shiny new values and mission statements; there needs to be executive investment, accountability, and commitment. Too often, conversations about Employee Experience and culture stall because they aren't integrated into how companies actually operate. We wrote this book to help change that.

We believe that when employees are empowered and supported to do the work that they are responsible for, great Employee Experience and culture are the inevitable by-products rather than the driving force. Rather than treating culture and experience as stand-alone goals, *WORK then PLACE* shows how they emerge from well-supported work. When employees are empowered to perform their jobs effectively, trust is built. When systems reinforce rather than obstruct, culture follows.

The goal of *WORK then PLACE* is to remind us that major change doesn't need to be intimidating or begin with big declarations and expensive overhauls. The truth is, it can start with small, measurable changes rooted in behavioral insight, led by teams that already understand what success in their work looks like. Executives and leaders don't have to carry the full burden. Your job is to define the goals, create structural guardrails, and extend trust to your teams to shape how work succeeds. That's because real change takes time and requires coordination, feedback, and care. But it's possible. Modern work is a team sport, and your workplace can be a powerful teammate.

We hope this book helps you move from friction to clarity, from short-term fixes to long-term capability. The goal isn't perfection. It's progress. In the words of Arthur Ashe: "Start where you are. Use what you have. Do what you can."

We'll begin by exploring how we arrived at this point and why designing modern work must precede redesigning our workplaces.

Corinne Murray
May 2025
Brooklyn and Long Island, NY

Sara Mailloux Escobar
May 2025
Los Angeles, CA & Portland, OR

SECTION ONE:

SETTING THE FOUNDATION

1

Building Blocks

What Shapes the Modern Workplace

Rethinking the workplace requires that we agree on what the term even means for the modern company and the modern worker. We must recalibrate foundational terms and distinctions for the twenty-first century that set the stage for how we make decisions today and in the future.

What Workplace Actually Is

The workplace is often reduced to an equivalent of "the office"—a container where work happens. But, in reality, it's an ecosystem that either accelerates or obstructs work. *WORK then PLACE* distinguishes the two essential components of the workplace: *WORK* (the behaviors that create value) and *PLACE* (the systems that support those behaviors). Understanding both—and how they relate—is key to making modern work and workplaces work.

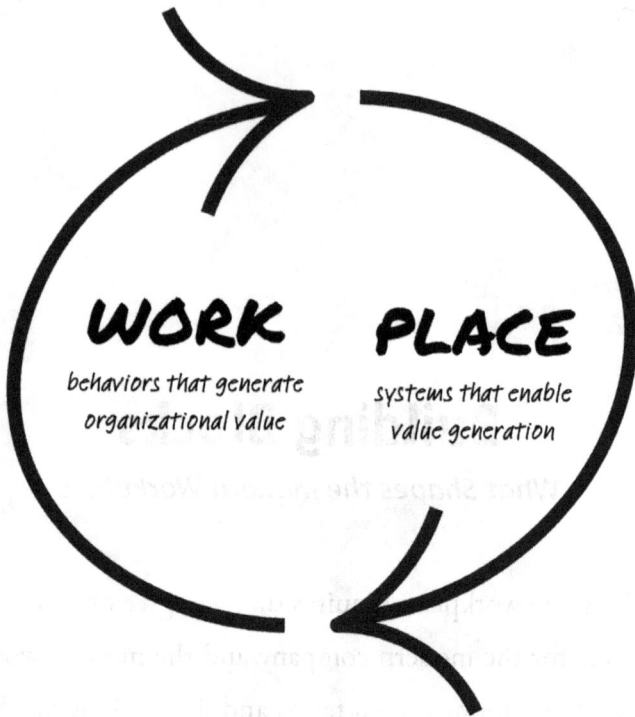

WORK
behaviors that generate
organizational value

PLACE
systems that enable
value generation

The *WORK* within workplace is just what it sounds like: The work contributing to a company's products and services that creates value and profit. Some work directly correlates with company profits, like product development, marketing, and sales. Some work is more indirect, such as talent acquisition, corporate communications, and business operations, but it creates specific conditions for the business to thrive. The *PLACE* within workplace enables how work is done within a company, ideally creating a flow and ease that fosters business success and a thriving company culture. This responsibility is far broader than what occurs within the four walls of an office.

The Three Environments of the Workplace

Because we can conceptualize and understand what is tactile more easily than the invisible and less tangible, it's understandable that we assume *PLACE* is limited to what we can see and touch. When we look more closely, however, we realize that today's working world would collapse if companies focused solely on the physical aspects of where and how work is done. Ultimately, *PLACE* is the unification of the physical, digital, and experiential environments.

Digital Environment

The infrastructure is where most work actually happens. Digital tools, platforms, and systems must enable practical, efficient workflows, regardless of where people are located.

Experiential Environment

The experiential dimension of the workplace—its policies, norms, rituals, and daily behaviors—is where strategy becomes reality. It's the space where values meet operations, and where ambiguity can either dissolve through clarity or deepen through neglect. This is also where the greatest opportunity for evolution lives.

Physical Environment

The physical places where work happens—offices, homes, coworking spaces, cafés, trains, airports, or wherever there's Wi-Fi and a power outlet. These spaces may vary in formality, but they remain essential to the overall experience. Physical environments shape behavior, send cultural signals, and define the edges of a team's shared reality.

In the most technical terms, the digital environment is the true default for where modern work and business happen. Regardless of whether a company requires significant in-office time or if teammates are working from anywhere in the world, the outputs of every knowledge work activity inevitably rely on the digital environment and the norms and policies shaped by the experiential environment that govern it.

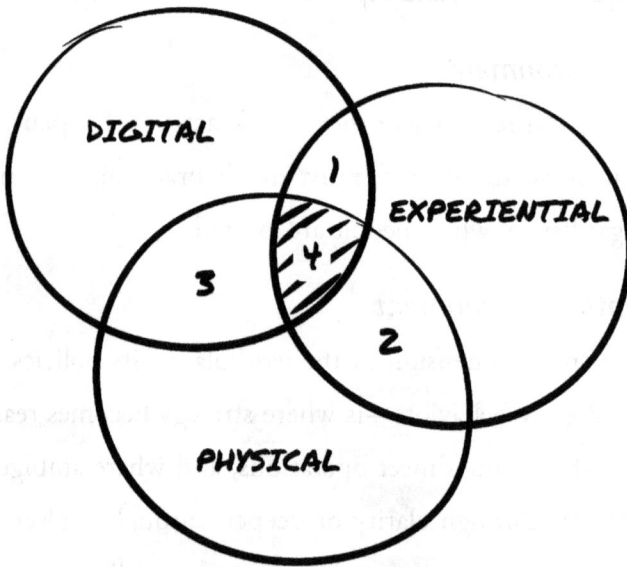

1. Workflow Enablement & Digital Rituals
2. Culture Signaling & Spatial Norms
3. Frictionless Access & Infrastructure Fluidity
4. Integrated & Holistic Workplace

A company's experiential environment is the ingredient that seamlessly blends the digital and physical into a unified and coherent ecosystem. Just as an emulsifier combines oil and vinegar into a smooth vinaigrette, the right experiential environment brings together your digital and physical workplaces into one cohesive whole. The quality of this emulsifier is where the essence of each company lives. Companies that invest in fortifying the connection between these three environments will create dynamic, resilient workplaces and workforces that can weather challenges long into the future.

Why Workplace Matters Now

Understanding the structure of the modern workplace is one thing. Recognizing why it matters right now—amid rapid shifts in work patterns, technologies, and employee expectations—is another.

The workplace's greatest challenge is that it has outgrown its roots, but still hasn't risen as high as it needs to on the list of priorities within companies. As a discipline, the workplace has primarily operated within the confines of a company's Real Estate & Facilities function, which has always been responsible for designing, building, and operating the office environment. However, as work became more mobile and digital, the boundaries of where the workplace begins and ends—literally and figuratively—became blurrier.

The workplace has evolved into a complex intersection of physical, digital, and experiential environments, and it is rare for the owners of these disciplines—Real Estate, HR, or IT—to make unified, holistic decisions about the workplace's maintenance and improvement. Due to its perception as a cost center rather than a profit enabler in the eyes of many executives, the workplace isn't often granted the authority or leadership necessary to facilitate a better Employee Experience and company success.

As a result, many Real Estate, HR, and IT professionals are unprepared to meet the demands of today's and tomorrow's workforce and workplace. As a result, practitioners must now undergo a rapid transition and upskill from supporting states of stability to developing and managing innovative strategies that redefine the human relationship to work, what resources teams need to be productive, and how the company continuously supports these activities. Unfortunately, the skills and mindsets required for the future stand in stark contrast to much of what currently exists within these disciplines.

Why Terms Matter & Where We've Gotten Them Wrong

Progress without shared language is an illusion. When teams or organizations use the same words to mean different things—or different words to mean the same thing—they build strategy on a shaky foundation. Misalignment in terminology breeds confusion, slows momentum, and increases risk to the longevity and functionality of a workplace.

To drive meaningful change in an organization's workplace, we must begin with clarity around historical definitions, nuanced interpretations, and overlapping domains that shape how workplace-related terms are used—and misused. Establishing a common language aids communication, anchors alignment, and helps teams make decisions with confidence, operate with consistency, and reduce the friction that comes from misinterpretation. Overall, precision and context are prerequisites, not nice-to-haves, for building systems that serve real needs and avoid imagined ones.

Workplace vs. Real Estate & Facilities

Once more, for the folks in the back, the workplace and Real Estate & Facilities are inextricably linked, but they are not the same thing.

Before the pandemic, most organizations operated under a clear assumption: Employees work in the office, and Real Estate & Facilities keep the offices running. However, that clarity and neat categorization to define workplace ownership is now gone.

Until 2020, remote work was rare. In 2021, the National Council of Compensation Insurance reported that 75 percent of knowledge workers had never worked from home before the pandemic *(National Council of Compensation Insurance and Coate 2021)*. Work happened in the offices that companies managed with the help of a highly visible facilities team. The inequities of headquarters versus regional offices having less access and presence were acknowledged but not pressing.

However, this broadened understanding of the workplace's scope beyond the physical environment did not happen overnight.

Two primary seeds of change in the United States were planted in the early 2000s: one was the replacement of desktop computers with laptops *(Hofstra Labor & Employment Law Journal and Schess 2013)*, the other was the telework movement of the 1980s and emergency remote work initiatives in the New York tri-State area following the events of September 11, 2001.

For better or worse, the concept of the workplace stretched its legs and took its first steps the moment work could be carried home in our backpacks or hands, embracing the mission to empower work from anywhere and everywhere. Then, in March 2020, the Great WFH Experiment began. Work continued, and the importance of the workplace's digital and experiential ecosystems came to the forefront.

Despite battling Zoom fatigue, a phenomenon validated by Yale Medical School in 2023, which found that the human brain experiences more stress while processing virtual interactions than it does while processing in-person ones, knowledge workers unlocked a newfound equity among colleagues that was previously irreconcilable in the pre-pandemic era. That's because work was happening on our screens, regardless of where our bodies were *(Zhao et al. 2023)*.

Employee Experience vs. Workplace Experience

Just as the workplace is often misunderstood, so are the terms tied to how employees interact with it. Workplace Experience is nested within Employee Experience, which is the full life cycle of an employee's (or prospective employee's) experience at any company.

However, Workplace Experience benefits align with employee programs, providing operational teams with a wide range of opportunities to create high-quality experiences that foster and support employee engagement and effectiveness.

We've chosen not to focus on employee benefits, such as healthcare, learning and development, parental leave, or paid time off, in this book. However, these programs are foundational benefits for employees and their families and ultimately affect the bigger picture. That's because if employees have negative experiences with their benefits, it impacts their overall satisfaction and ultimately hurts both the company and the quality of work produced.

To simplify:

- **Workplace Experience** is centered around the tools, ecosystems, and systems required to support employees and their work.

- **Employee Experience** encompasses the comprehensive relationship that employees have with the companies they represent.

These two practices often get confused or conflated because, in most circumstances, the stakeholders are the same. While Workplace, HR, IT, and Operations teams are responsible for architecting these experience frameworks, they must be defined separately to maximize potential and power. As part of the *WORK then PLACE* processes, defining what resources are needed for what parts of the experience is imperative to success.

Experience vs. Culture

Experience—including Workplace and Employee Experience—is a key ingredient of a company's culture. However, culture is not merely a sum of experiences. Rather, culture is shaped by how those experiences are absorbed, repeated, and shared across the organization. Although experience and culture are often used interchangeably in business discussions, they are interdependent.

The experiences that employees have while working at a company, whether intentionally designed or an organizational blind spot, contribute to a company's culture. When companies design experiences for employees, the inputs, outputs, and resources needed for success are measurable, tangible, and something you can point to. Culture, on the other hand, is amorphous and constantly shapeshifting in response to the intentionally designed or passively established employee experiences within an organization.

In the article, "Culture and Quality: An Anthropological Perspective," Patricia Hudelson writes:

> "Most anthropologists would define culture as the shared set of (implicit and explicit) values, ideas, concepts, and rules of behavior that allow a social group to function and perpetuate itself. Rather than simply the presence or absence of a particular attribute, culture is understood as the dynamic and evolving socially constructed reality that exists in the minds of social group members. The 'normative glue' allows group members to communicate and work effectively together." *(Hudelson 2004, 345–346)*

Employee Experience is the core component of a company's "normative glue," connecting disparate aspects of a company into a single entity. Our struggle to define experience and its influence on decision-making throughout an organization is one of the primary reasons we've faced so much workplace strife in the past four years.

A company's culture is best understood as Employee Experience on the grandest scale. Culture is the accumulation of experiences from hundreds, if not thousands, of employees across an organization, each with different titles, responsibilities, and pay grades. *WORK then PLACE* insists that we make these implicit and occasionally unconscious behaviors explicit and visible. From this place of awareness, we can evaluate how these behaviors shape a company's culture and clarify what changes must happen and why.

British psychologist John Amaechi defines culture as the collection of "worst behaviors tolerated" within a group *(WorkLife, Grant, and Amaechi 2021)*. Disempowering employees with negative or unhelpful experiences that they cannot change or improve affects a company's culture and, ultimately, damages its bottom line. We must embrace the idea that culture comes from building, measuring, and iterating experiences. Our efforts to improve work experiences will help represent the culture rather than define it.

Experiencing v. Remembering

The most effective approach to designing experiences is to reduce friction and minimize interferences. Although designing universally positive and memorable experiences is the goal, it's also a pipe dream. Pulling inspiration from Daniel Kahneman's *Thinking Fast and Slow*, we recommend starting by designing away from bad experiences rather than designing toward good experiences.

That's because good experiences are highly personal and subjective, whereas bad experiences are more universal. The characteristics of one person's good day can be radically different from those of another, while annoyances, inconveniences, and larger challenges are more relatable. The universality of bad experiences helps us create broad-reaching strategies and solutions that elevate the overall experience for everyone.

This critical nuance anchors us back to the importance of designing for needs rather than preferences. Thanks to the amygdala, our brains are wired to bookmark the bad stuff with more precision and detail than the good, a throwback to our cave-dwelling days when remembering which berries were toxic kept us from becoming dinner. This ancient alarm system now tends to misfire cues in our modern-day operating system more often than not.

When we discuss experience in the modern workplace, we're talking about the efforts to design and sustain experiences that people don't remember for all the best reasons: seamlessness, ease, and intuitiveness. As you think about creating your company's Workplace Experience, define what you are trying to achieve. It likely isn't just about "getting work done." Creating opportunities for employees to connect, collaborate, innovate, and inspire is an essential element of a memorable Workplace Experience. Above all else, teams must always have a keen eye for the inconveniences and frustrations that could eclipse the winning aspects of the Employee Experience.

Preferences vs. Requirements

To best evaluate Employee and Workplace Experience, and the cultures they foster, we need to examine the ingredients and their qualities honestly. For example, many employee experiences are designed to generate individual happiness and moments of surprise and delight, without establishing a direct correlation to an organization's overall objectives. When we focus on accommodating preferences (what we like) instead of fulfilling requirements (what we need), we create consumer-driven experiences instead of effectiveness-driven ones. Once clarified, these distinctions help teams focus their energy on what's actionable, impactful, and scalable.

When discussing the critical differences between preferences and requirements, we can draw parallels to Maslow's Hierarchy of Needs, the American psychologist's interpretation of aspects of the indigenous Siksika or Blackfoot way of life, first published in 1943 *(GatherFor and Ravilochan 2021)*. Using Maslow's philosophy as a guiding framework, employee requirements are most suitably compared to the physiological and safety needs at the bottom of the pyramid. In contrast, employee preferences are most closely aligned with esteem and self-actualization at the top of the pyramid. But executives often mistrust the financial benefits of Employee and Workplace Experience initiatives because they lack alignment with the organization's performance goals or are geared more toward the upper levels of Maslow's pyramid.

MASLOW'S HIERARCHY OF NEEDS

REALITY

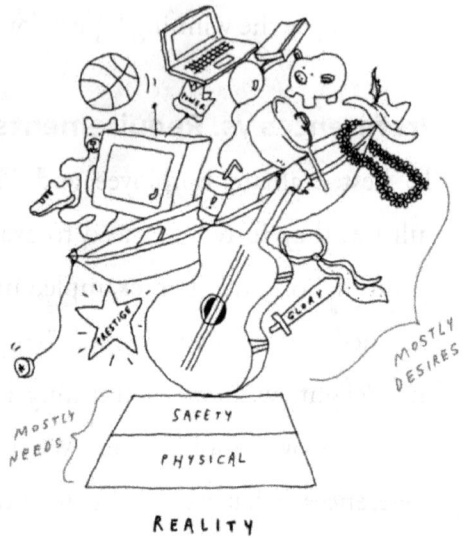

Illustration credit: Liana Finck

Providing nursing parents' rooms, incorporating accommodations for workers with special needs, distributing branded swag, fostering a healthy meeting culture, and hosting company parties are all elements of a comprehensive Workplace Experience strategy. However, the elements that yield the greatest benefit require the greatest investment, deterring many companies from making such investments.

The Rise of the Workplace Strategist

The need to understand these nuances and necessary evolutions in the workplace has given rise to a new kind of leader; someone who can build the bridge for workplaces and organizations to move from legacy, office-centric traditions focused on stability, to modern and future-prepared ecosystems that strive for agility and dynamism through systems thinking and human-centered design. These leaders are the Workplace Strategists. Improving modern work requires analyzers, visionaries, tinkerers, and systems thinkers with a keen eye for human behavior, historical context, and a restless drive to leave people, places, and practices better than they found them. However, there's no direct academic path to this work, which leaves the door open for anyone curious enough to walk through it and introduce themselves to the ever-evolving intersection of modern work. The fact that Workplace Strategists gravitate toward a discipline that mimics their habit of constant growth and evolution is pure coincidence and fate.

WORK then PLACE aims to awaken the Workplace Strategist in all of us. You don't need a formal title to be one. You need curiosity, care, and a commitment to better ways of working for yourself and others.

Building Blocks: What Shapes the Workplace

The Rise of the Workplace Strategist

The Shift to Understand the Employee Experience

The Workplace as Caregiver

The Workplace as Provider

2

In Practice

How Workplaces Impact Us

The workplace is not just where work happens—it's how work happens. It's the coordinated system that turns behaviors into business outcomes, encompassing physical tools, digital systems, and social experience.

Workplaces as Relationship Hubs

A healthy relationship with work is built on more than just what people are responsible for in their jobs. How they're supported while they're doing it—by workplace systems, the broader organization, and each other—holds a lot of weight in whether one's relationship to work feels successful or not. These supports form the foundation of workplace relationships, connecting individuals to their teams, tools, leaders, and a broader sense of purpose. When thoughtfully designed, the workplace evolves from a site of productivity into a multidimensional hub for trust, collaboration, and mutual growth.

These relationships aren't housed in a single channel. They stretch across physical, digital, and experiential environments—and thrive only when those environments function as a cohesive system. When they're aligned, they amplify each other; the digital tools that enable collaboration also reinforce expectations shaped in the experiential layer, while the physical environment serves as a signal of culture, inclusion, and care.

The three workplace ecosystems—physical, digital, and experiential—are nonnegotiable components of any modern workplace. Whether your company operates remotely, in the office, or somewhere in between, success depends on understanding how these environments interact and making the necessary investments to support them.

Cross-functional collaboration and informal connections don't happen by accident. They require conditions that support chance encounters, shared context, and accessible systems. Physical environments shape how and where people meet, gather, and exchange ideas, while digital environments extend those relationships across time and geography, providing teams with continuity beyond the physical room. Experiential systems—such as norms, rituals, communication, and feedback loops—build the trust and clarity that make all interactions meaningful.

It is when these three environments disconnect that relationships break down. Then people struggle to locate each other, expectations feel mismatched, and feedback loops falter. But when these layers work in harmony, they form a resilient foundation for multidirectional relationships between functions, levels, locations, and personalities.

Workplaces are not battlegrounds or compliance zones; they are ecosystems of interdependence, where connection is a condition for performance and well-being. Overall, strong workplaces cultivate the networks—formal and informal—that help teams navigate ambiguity, respond to change, and build something better together.

The Systems Behind Every Experience

The workplace is not a backdrop—it's a living system that choreographs how work unfolds. It's where operations and experience intersect in real time. Yet, historically, companies have approached workplace decisions in silos, segmenting real estate, technology, and culture into separate domains. We have found that that division no longer works.

To understand how physical, digital, and experiential systems operate in tandem, consider a familiar setting: a restaurant. Every restaurant is a live, multidimensional system where distinct roles and tools must work in sync to create a seamless experience. The front-of-house team—hosts, servers, bartenders, and managers—shapes the experiential environment by orchestrating tone, timing, and interaction. Their success depends on customer service and interpersonal skills as well as clear norms, a shared language, and a culture of service. They are the face of the experience, and they define how customers feel.

Behind the scenes, the back-of-house team—chefs, line cooks, dishwashers, and prep staff—relies on a finely tuned physical environment. Their tools, layouts, and workflows determine what's possible, and well-designed stations, equipment, and handoff zones create the infrastructure that supports quality, safety, and speed. Meanwhile, the digital environment ties everything together. Point-of-sale platforms, ticketing systems, inventory tracking, and scheduling software create the connective tissue. They ensure that the right inputs reach the right people at the right time—and that data flows back through the system to inform future decisions.

The three systems are distinct, but inseparable. A restaurant cannot function with just great ambiance, excellent food, or efficient tech. Success depends on shared standards, clean handoffs, and continuous feedback across all three layers. This is how modern workplaces must operate. The experiential layer defines the cultural tone and behavioral expectations. The physical layer provides the infrastructure that enables these behaviors. The digital layer coordinates, records, and reinforces them. When these systems are aligned and mutually aware, organizations can deliver an experience that works, from the inside out.

That's the task of workplace strategy in the twenty-first century: To broaden and diversify the tools used to ignite workplace transformation. Companies—and those who lead them—must update assumptions about modern work and reimagine how tasks are accomplished. Doing so opens the door to workflows that not only meet business needs but also improve the Employee Experience.

If this book achieves only one thing, let it be this: Workplaces only succeed when the distinct but integrated layers of place actively support the core components of work. Historically, workplace design has failed to connect productivity, effectiveness, and culture to measurable business outcomes. It's time to change that.

Promoting effective work is about more than increasing operational efficiency or employee output. It means connecting visible tasks and workflows with the less tangible elements: the tools, resources, group dynamics, and cultural signals that shape how work happens.

With this holistic view—supported by both quantitative and qualitative data—we get a real snapshot of how the system is performing. Strategy can't rely on instinct or seniority alone. It must be informed by how the full system actually functions, not just how we imagine it should.

Five Generations, Five Expectations

Today's workforce spans five generations, each shaped by different economic conditions, technologies, and cultural norms. From Traditionalists to Gen Z, and soon Gen Alpha, these cohorts bring deeply distinct expectations to the workplace. Research from Johns Hopkins University describes the priorities of each generation:

Traditionalists/Silent Generation
Disciplined, resilient, and rooted in hierarchy, Traditionalists value stability and professionalism. They tend to be self-reliant but may struggle to ask for help.

Baby Boomers
Competitive and work-centric, Boomers often prioritize efficiency

and performance over work-life balance, viewing career advancement as a linear climb.

Gen X

Independent and adaptable, Gen Xers value autonomy, flexibility, and informal work environments. They often strive for a balance between work and life while embracing technological advancements.

Gen Y/Millennials

Purpose-driven and adaptable, Millennials seek out opportunities for growth, inclusivity, and personal development. They expect the organizations they represent to embody transparency, equity, and social responsibility.

Gen Z

Growing up online in an increasingly digital world, Gen Z questions traditional structures and demands ethical clarity. They prioritize environments that offer honest communication, mental health support, and purposeful work. *(Lee and Johns Hopkins University 2022)*

Generation	Born	% of the US workforce in 2025
Traditionalists/Silent Gen	1925–1945	>1%
Baby Boomers	1946–1964	15%
Gen X	1965–1980	31%
Gen Y/Millennials	1981–1996	36%
Gen Z	1997–2012	~8%
Gen Alpha	2010–2025	N/A

(US Department of Labor 2024)

These generational norms highlight more than just personal preferences; they illuminate how individuals respond to systems, change, and leadership. For Traditionalists, Boomers, and many Gen Xers, work followed a predictable pattern: loyalty, hierarchy, and linear progression. However, Millennials and Gen Z entered a world defined by volatility, demanding a different kind of workplace—one rooted in purpose, care, and adaptability.

The tension? Many senior leaders today are Boomers or Gen Xers who may resist abandoning models that once worked. Meanwhile, younger employees expect transparency and transformation. This disconnect can erode trust, particularly when changes are poorly explained or inconsistently applied.

Why One Office Can't Fit All

The evolution of office design reveals how generational experiences have diverged, and why aligning expectations today is so difficult.

Private Offices and Power

Traditionalists, Baby Boomers, and older Gen Xers often began their careers in workplaces defined by closed doors and corner offices. These spaces weren't just functional—they were status symbols. Visibility, control, and seniority were embedded into the floor plan.

The Open Office Shift

In the aughts, many Gen Xers were midcareer when the financial crisis demanded cost-saving strategies. All the while, open-plan designs became the norm, promising flexibility and collaboration. Millennials entered during this shift and largely normalized open seating, even if they didn't love it. By the late 2010s, critiques of open offices were widespread: distractions were high, privacy was low, and productivity suffered as a result.

Gen Z and the Remote First

Gen Z entered the workforce around 2017. Then came the COVID-19 pandemic. For many, the traditional office was short-lived or entirely absent. Their formative work experiences were virtual, distributed, and self-directed—more assumptions than memories. Expectations of flexibility, inclusivity, and well-being were formed in the absence of legacy norms.

The result? One office may host up to five generations, each with five different interpretations of what a normal Workplace Experience looks like, making the workplace no longer a neutral backdrop. As a result, the workplace is now a contested space shaped by memory, power, preference, and purpose. Understanding these generational lenses is key to designing systems that work not just for some but better for everyone.

The modern workplace is no longer one-size-fits-all, if it ever truly was. With five generations working side by side, shaped by different eras, technologies, and economic conditions, no single environment or system can meet every expectation on its own. So, what makes today's workplace functional and fair isn't uniformity—it's integration.

When the physical, digital, and experiential layers operate in harmony, they create the infrastructure for connection across differences in age, identity, style, and expectations, and thus make collaboration scalable, trust durable, and performance sustainable. But when those layers are misaligned—when systems are designed in isolation or shaped by a single generation's memory—friction grows, relationships fray, and engagement declines.

The workplace is a bit like Rome: all roads lead to it. And, like Rome, pizza is surprisingly easy to come by. But more importantly, everything an organization values—its culture, operations, tools, and relationships—eventually converges in the workplace. If that convergence is thoughtful and aligned, the workplace becomes more than a setting. It becomes a system that helps people and businesses thrive. For example, a workplace built for the future must acknowledge its past without being beholden to it. The corner office isn't the only symbol of success anymore, the open floor plan isn't the only path to collaboration, and remote work isn't just a contingency—it's a legitimate mode of working that must be intentionally supported.

This is the promise of workplace strategy today: to connect the core components of work with the full spectrum of human experience and ensure that how we work and where we work are designed not just for efficiency, but for belonging, clarity, and growth. The chapters ahead will demonstrate how to achieve this by aligning workplace ecosystems with organizational purpose and transforming environments into enablers of effective and equitable work.

3

Under the Hood

The Mechanics of Modern Work

Seeing that the nature of modern work is dynamic and ever-changing, it is no wonder that it often outpaces the systems intended to support it. Therefore, meaningfully improving these systems begins with understanding the behaviors that shape our work and questioning whether traditional measures of productivity still apply.

Here, modern work refers not just to the present-day realities of how work gets done, but to the full arc of transformation that has shaped—and will continue to shape—how businesses operate. It encompasses both what is happening now and what is on the horizon: the emerging patterns, pressures, and possibilities that demand new ways of thinking, working, and leading.

Modern Work & the Future of Work

Compared to the nebulous and overused "future of work" concept, *WORK then PLACE* focuses on addressing the challenges of modern work because change is needed now, not later. But the relationship between modern work and the future of work is deep and inextricable, and many experts will mention one while inherently referencing the other.

The future of work is best understood as a continuum that extends beyond the current boundaries of what is possible. It dares us to imagine work beyond today's constraints and consider what could become a reality in the years to come. In contrast, modern work challenges us to make those possibilities a reality now. Simultaneously, as modern work's capabilities continuously expand, it ups the ante on how and where the future of work can evolve.

On its own, the phrase "future of work" can seem esoteric and detached, making it challenging to define its broad scope with enough precision to motivate action. Talking about the future without anchoring it in the present gives unspoken permission to delay action and treat change as optional rather than essential. It allows too many to defer the responsibility for the future away from ourselves and toward the next cohort of leaders or, perhaps, the technology that is to come.

Instead, the path to the future is paved by today's leaders through incremental shifts and changes that create durable infrastructure for transformation. We must understand that while technology plays a substantial role in shaping the future of work, it is not the primary driver of this change. People are. Every industrial and agricultural revolution throughout human history has been shaped by the tools and technologies we've built for ourselves. However, without transforming mindsets and behaviors—individually and organizationally—new tools will only streamline old problems rather than unlock new opportunities for employees and businesses. Today, most companies are struggling to meet the basic standards required of modern work, rendering entire industries and labor ecosystems unsustainable and in need of urgent attention.

Employee Wellness in Modern Work

In 2023, digital meditation and wellness company Calm released a report on mental health trends and the future of work, stating that "stress, burnout, loneliness, and anxiousness have skyrocketed, and mental health is now at the top of every employer's priority list" *(Calm Business 2023)*. Based on a 2022 user survey of over 2,000 people, primarily from the United States, concerns regarding isolation, lack of connection, and work performance increased significantly in just two years since the start of the COVID-19 pandemic. Nearly 70 percent of survey respondents said that employee mental health and wellness should be sponsored and supported by companies.

In a July 2024 report from The Upwork Research Institute, nearly three-quarters of full-time employees reported being burned out, and roughly two-thirds reported struggling with employer demands for more productivity *(Monahan, Burlacu, and Upwork 2024)*. One in three employees said they will likely quit their jobs within the next six months because they are burned out and overworked. Meanwhile, in the same report, over 80 percent of global C-suite leaders acknowledged the increased demands on their workforces in the past year, yet still believed that their companies prioritize employee well-being over productivity.

In addition to traditional compensation and benefits packages, some companies, many of which are large enterprises, offer a suite of perks and programs to support employees' day-to-day lives. Access to wellness offerings, such as subsidized gym memberships, mental health counseling, meditation services like Calm, nutritional coaching, legal and financial advice, and in-office food programs, are among the common premium offerings that supplement the compensation packages for corporate employees. Although wellness programs signal good intentions from employers, access alone isn't enough to derive value. If these offerings aren't integrated into how the business operates, they often remain unused and ineffective. Overall, employee wellness has historically been treated as an individualized issue that lives outside of the company's core. As a result, we are often blindsided by the systemic challenges that arise when employee wellness is in a state of distress. The evidence of employee wellness crises, especially among knowledge workers, has been evident even before the COVID-19 pandemic, but little structural change has occurred to improve employee wellness.

This disconnect between executive perceptions and the lived experiences of employees lies at the heart of the modern work crisis. Until wellness is treated as a core input to employee productivity and effectiveness, organizations and their workforces will remain trapped in cycles of burnout, attrition, and underperformance.

The State of Work Today & Progress for Tomorrow

Knowledge work is a prominent, but poorly defined, component of the corporate landscape today. This ambiguity affects how companies measure productivity, design policies, and support employees. Around the world, these workers report rising stress, cognitive overload, and a widening gap between what they need and what their workplaces provide. Distinct from other types of labor that require more physical engagement, like trade and manual labor, knowledge workers are more susceptible to these specific workplace strains.

HP Work Relationship Index (% of knowledge workers who have a healthy relationship with work)

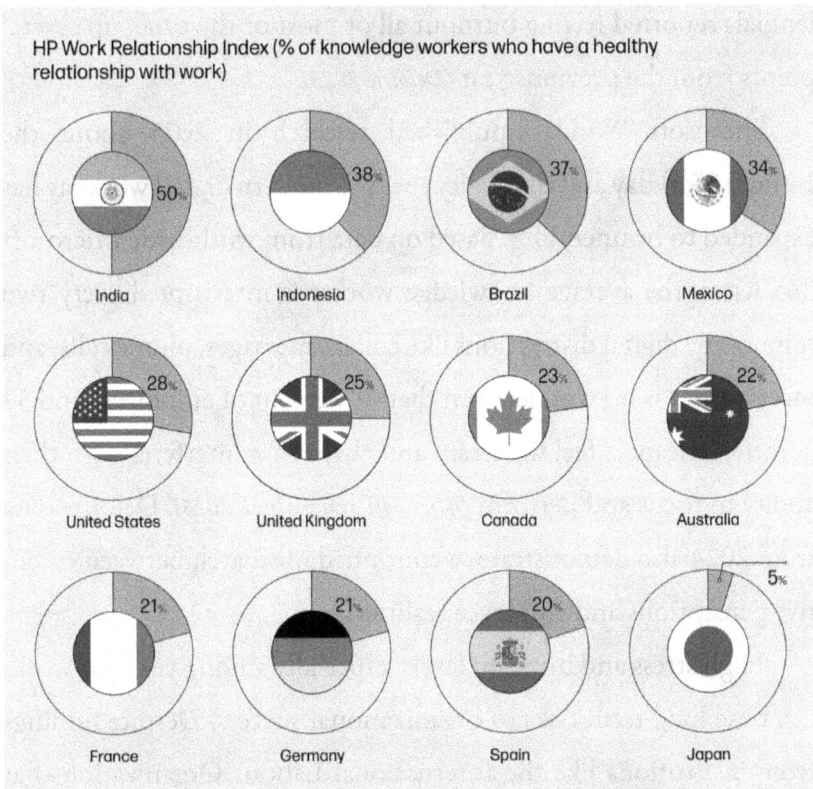

India	Indonesia	Brazil	Mexico
50%	38%	37%	34%

United States	United Kingdom	Canada	Australia
28%	25%	23%	22%

France	Germany	Spain	Japan
21%	21%	20%	5%

Mounting research confirms that our relationship with work, especially in the United States, is misaligned with the demands of modern life. In HP's 2023 Work Relationship Index, knowledge workers across twelve major economies struggle to access even one of six core drivers of healthy work: Fulfillment, Leadership, People Centricity, Skills, Tools, and Workspace.

Markets like Japan, Spain, Germany, and France reported especially poor work relationships. The United States fared only slightly better, scoring just above the global average of 27 percent. In short, what we've built isn't working *(HP 2023)*. A Deloitte survey from the same year found that 52 percent of Gen Z and 49 percent of millennials reported feeling burnout all or most of the time, up several points from the previous year *(Deloitte 2023)*.

Microsoft Worklab published research in 2025 about the Infinite Workday and the reality that the modern digital workday has expanded to be unending. Based on data from worldwide Microsoft 365 users, the average knowledge worker is interrupted every two minutes by digital distractions like emails, messages, phone calls, and meetings. It is no wonder then that 48 percent of employees and 52 percent of leaders feel the strain and chaos that interferes with their ability to focus and perform *(Microsoft and Galván 2025)*. Deloitte data from 2024 also demonstrates a continued mismatch between executive perceptions and employee realities.

High stress and burnout levels, especially among younger workers, pose long-term risks to organizational success. Despite findings from institutions like the International Labour Organization that

The modern work experience doesn't promote human sustainability. But C-suite leaders aren't seeing it.

● Workers who selected "always" or "often"   ○ C-suite who selected "always" or "often"

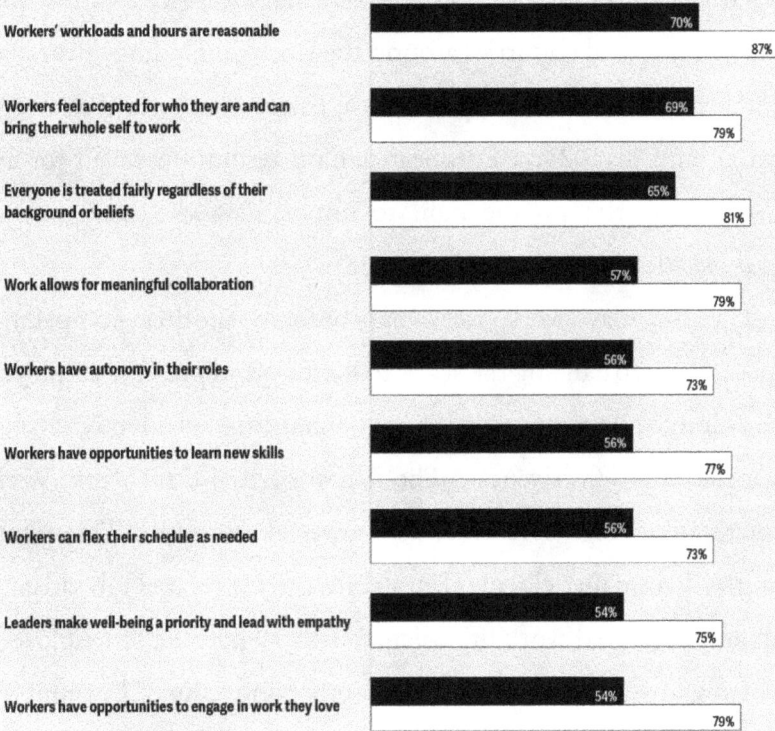

	Workers	C-suite
Workers' workloads and hours are reasonable	70%	87%
Workers feel accepted for who they are and can bring their whole self to work	69%	79%
Everyone is treated fairly regardless of their background or beliefs	65%	81%
Work allows for meaningful collaboration	57%	79%
Workers have autonomy in their roles	56%	73%
Workers have opportunities to learn new skills	56%	77%
Workers can flex their schedule as needed	56%	73%
Leaders make well-being a priority and lead with empathy	54%	75%
Workers have opportunities to engage in work they love	54%	79%

Source: Deloitte 2024 Well-being at Work survey.

Deloitte Insights | deloitte.com/insights

longer working hours can counteract productivity, 66 percent of CEOs recognize that change is needed but are still reluctant to pursue work models and approaches that differ from what is familiar *(World Economic Forum and Thesing 2023; Accenture et al. 2022).* As a result, some regions are responding to these business realities on behalf of their citizens.

Starting in France in 2016, Right to Disconnect laws began to limit the expectations of off-work hours that companies could otherwise legally place on their workers *(Axios and Peck 2024)*. In the years since, several countries around the world, including Australia, Kazakhstan, and the Philippines, have passed similar universal legislation, and in 2021, a European Union resolution called for an EU-wide directive on the right to unplug *(World Economic Forum, Wood, and Shine 2023)*.

The four-day work week has become another compelling approach to rebalancing the scales to increase and preserve employee well-being while preserving, if not enhancing, productivity and organizational effectiveness. The UK's 2022 4-Day Work Week pilot reported higher revenue and lower absenteeism. This pilot, along with a smaller global pilot, significantly increased job satisfaction and improved work-life balance with 39 percent of employees reporting lower stress and 71 percent reporting reduced burnout by the trial's end. In addition, 92 percent of the firms that participated in the study opted to continue using the 4-Day Work Week *(4 Day Week Global 2023)*.

Though such laws benefit all workers, they're especially relevant to knowledge workers, whose jobs can travel with them, thanks to mobile devices. Codifying norms and expectations around "on-hours" and "off-hours" gives cognitive labor the same rest and recovery periods that are understood as essential for physical labor. Yet compared to the rest of the world, legal protections and shifts to hours worked each week in the United States have been slower to emerge. California and New Jersey are the only two states that have introduced right-to-unplug legislation, but neither bill has passed yet due to tensions between business needs and employee well-being *(Atlas 2025)*. The first effort to introduce a four-day work-week to the United States came from then-Vice President Richard Nixon, but stalled in the late 1960s and did not reemerge until 2023, when California Representative Mark Takano introduced a bill for a thirty-two-hour workweek, which was later supported by Senators Laphonza Butler and Bernie Sanders. The goal: to give Americans more time to "live, play, and enjoy life fully outside of work" *(Takano 2023)*.

Although legislation for the right to unplug and shorter work-weeks has yet to progress, rising labor activism and pro-union sentiment among Americans could accelerate long-overdue labor reforms in the years to come *(Economic Policy Institute, Sojourner, and Reich 2025)*. Whatever future progress is made in the United States will be built on the foundation of earlier labor movements. Union organizers once fought to protect workers from physical dangers in the workplace, grueling seventy-hour manual labor workweeks, and unsafe environments. Today, the harms caused by persistent cognitive overload are the next frontier of worker safety. Growing awareness and advocacy around these modern labor needs will create the changes needed for knowledge workers to thrive more easily in the future.

Knowledge Work

In 1959, Peter Drucker, an Austrian-American businessman, educator, and author, coined the term "knowledge worker," and posited, "The most valuable asset of a twenty-first-century institution, whether business or non-business, will be its knowledge workers and their productivity" *(Drucker 1959)*. Sixty-five years later, this partly rings true. Knowledge workers and their productivity are essential to each company's operation, even if it's not the primary revenue generator. The greatest issue with this truth is that, despite the best efforts of businesses, economists, academics, and others, there is no common understanding and agreement on what knowledge work is, who does it, and how to measure productivity successfully.

Knowledge workers are those who are tasked with "non-routine" problem-solving that requires critical analysis and interpretation, creativity, and mental agility to make decisions when a clearly defined path is unavailable. Distinct from other types of workers, like information workers who focus on gathering, managing, and distributing information and data, knowledge workers take that information and translate it into new insights, strategies, products, and more *(IBM Education 2023)*.

Even workers who aren't technically classified as knowledge workers are likely to do similar work tasks. According to a 2023 paper from the International Labour Office, economists estimate that there are between 644 and 997 million knowledge work jobs, representing between 19.6 percent and 30.4 percent of global employment, respectively *(International Labour Office, Berg, and Gmyrek 2023)*. How these numbers shift in the coming years due to AI remains to be seen. Still, the prevailing theory is that the tasks workers are responsible for are becoming increasingly complex, requiring even more of the cognitive skills characteristic of knowledge work.

At its best, knowledge work offers flexibility, creativity, and economic mobility. As the modern iteration of white-collar work—a term credited by labor activist Upton Sinclair—it has long been associated with socioeconomic privilege. But, without proper guardrails, it is defined by round-the-clock availability, blurred boundaries, and chronic burnout that threatens both employee well-being and organizational performance *(Iskander 2018, 325–32)*. Traditional productivity metrics, designed for routine physical labor, fail to account for the cognitive and relational complexity that this work demands. That's because context specificity and siloed knowledge make it difficult to define and measure success in knowledge work. While this diversity adds value, it also obscures shared patterns, limiting strategic clarity. Without establishing a shared understanding of how work is done in companies and what support people need to perform their jobs effectively, these problems will persist. Therefore, we need some common ground on which to build.

To do so, we must broaden our perspective rather than narrow it. Leaders must zoom out from the subjectivity and specificity of the knowledge work within their discipline and identify the universal experiences that this type of work entails, regardless of industry or niche. Identifying and evaluating knowledge work from a broader vantage point is key to understanding its universal behaviors, moving us one step closer to measuring success and determining what is needed to create more of it.

The DNA of Knowledge Work

Knowledge work functions across four universal work modes regardless of industry, discipline, or location. These modes reflect not what the work is, but how it happens. They account for whether a task is solo or shared, planned or spontaneous, and whether it requires simultaneous attention from others.

Individual Focus

Work done alone, requiring concentration and autonomy.

Synchronous Collaboration

Real-time work with others, such as meetings or live co-creation.

Asynchronous Collaboration

Shared work that happens across different times, like commenting on a document or managing a shared task board.

Socializing

Interactions that build trust, expose teams to new ideas, and strengthen cross-functional relationships. Often informal, socializing supports the other three modes by fostering cohesion, creativity, and shared context.

together

SOCIALIZING

SYNCHRONOUS
COLLABORATION

organic ← → structured

INDIVIDUAL
FOCUS

ASYNCHRONOUS
COLLABORATION

solo

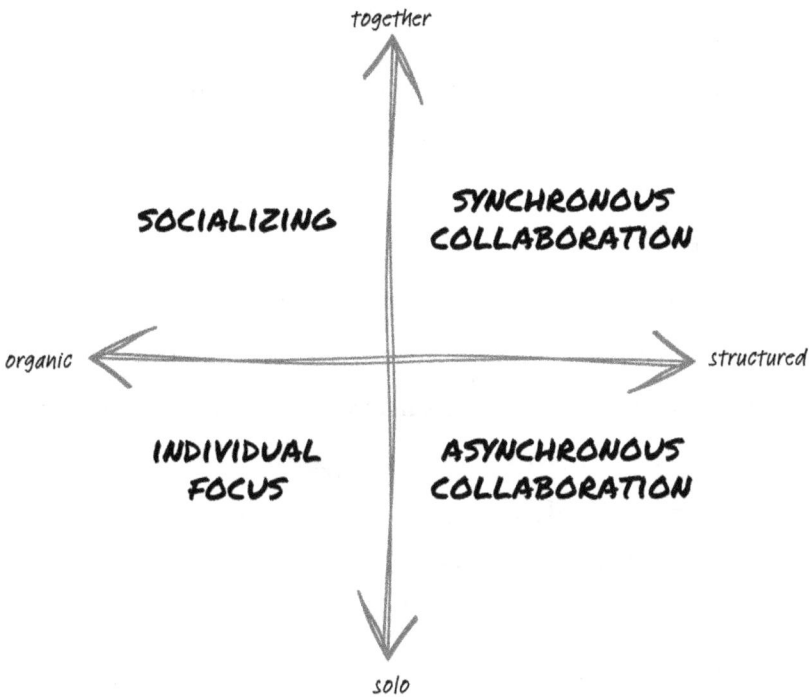

Credit: C. Murray & S. Escobar

These four modes provide a flexible framework for understanding how time is spent at the individual, team, and organizational levels, creating a shared language to identify work patterns and friction across disciplines and industries. As a result, working with this framework helps make less visible aspects of knowledge work, such as individual focus and socializing, more standardized and concrete, offering teams and leaders a way to articulate and support the full spectrum of modern work. However, because knowledge work is shaped by context and expertise, its outputs are harder to quantify. Yet, the behavioral foundations—focus, collaboration, and social connection—are universal. That consistency allows for better strategy, smarter measurement, and more aligned design, even across diverse teams and industries.

Socializing is often undervalued or misunderstood among the four modes of knowledge work. It's treated as extracurricular or disruptive to productivity when, in fact, it's the connective tissue that ensures the other three modes function in harmony. Socializing enables teams to stay aligned, share context, and challenge ideas early, preventing misalignment that can lead to rework or missed opportunities. While events and off-sites may support Employee Experience at a high level with day-to-day socializing, structural encouragement, and support. Stanford sociologist Mark Granovetter's work on "The Strength of Weak Ties" shows how informal relationships drive innovation and opportunity *(Granovetter and Johns Hopkins University 1973)*. In organizations, weak ties—such as cross-functional connections, informal chats, and chance encounters—often reveal critical insights and pathways for learning.

Despite executive appetite for innovation and collaboration, few companies build infrastructure to sustain these relational dynamics. This matrix provides leaders with a blueprint of the experiences required within their organizations to enable success at both the individual and business levels, serving as an audit tool that helps teams understand which experiences need more support.

Redefining Productivity & All Its Friends

Unlike other work types with clear, repeatable milestones, knowledge work is inherently subjective, making traditional output-based metrics unreliable. These traditional metrics fail to capture the full range of conditions that influence whether a person or team can perform at their best.

Today's productivity metrics still echo Ford's assembly-line logic, breaking work into repeatable tasks optimized for output *(Willamette University, n.d.)*. While often attributed to Frederick Taylor, much of today's linear, output-focused thinking stems from Ford's assembly-line model, which broke work into repeatable tasks to maximize efficiency and reduce costs *(Taylor 1903)*. However, knowledge work is dynamic and nonlinear, making it inherently incompatible with this measurement approach and requiring more adaptive ways to assess performance. Unlike roles with clear, repeatable outputs, knowledge work is subjective, nonuniform, and context dependent. As a result, many workers' roles have been broadened beyond formal job descriptions and involve more "invisible" cognitive tasks. However, this reality clashes with traditional productivity metrics that executives still rely on and, instead of creating quality outcomes for the organization, employees feel pressured to "perform" productivity on average 32 percent of their time *(Deloitte, Commisso, and Cantrell 2023)*.

A landmark 2014 report by Advanced Workplace Associates' (AWA) Workplace Performance Innovation Network reviewed over 800 academic studies to identify what drives the productivity of knowledge workers *(AWA Performance Innovation Network 2014)*. The six key factors are: Social Cohesion, Trust, Perceived Support, Information Sharing, External Communications, Vision, and Goal Clarity.

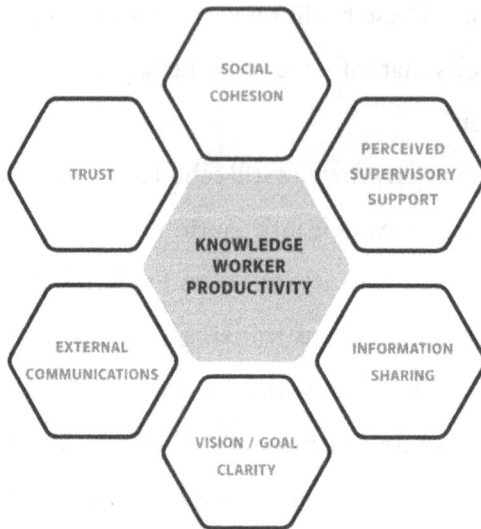

Credit to: AWA Workplace Performance Innovation Network

Notably absent were individual motivation techniques or top-down performance mandates. Instead, the findings pointed squarely at organizational structure, relationships, and clarity of purpose. In other words, productivity is a systems issue, not just a personal one.

Despite this, many leaders still rely on Ford-esque productivity data to make decisions, often conflating presence with performance. In a 2023 Slack Survey, 60 percent of executives say they track everything from hours worked and mouse activity to the number of emails sent to gauge the productivity of their workforce, despite only 15 percent of employees agreeing that this kind of monitoring helps them achieve more *(Slack 2023)*. But productivity is only the visible tip of the iceberg of a company's ability to generate revenue and value. Beneath it lie culture, systems, processes, and expectations—the true determinants of whether high-quality work can happen at scale.

Successfully supporting knowledge work requires prioritizing effectiveness over productivity. Effectiveness combines the effort of creating output with the experience of producing it. It accounts for what gets done and how it's accomplished, whether the approach is sustainable, repeatable, and proportionate to the effort required.

$$\textbf{PRODUCTIVITY} + \textbf{EXPERIENCE} = \textbf{EFFECTIVENESS}$$

$$\left(\begin{array}{c} \underline{OUTPUT} \\ INPUT \end{array} \right) \qquad \left(INTERDEPENDENCIES \right) \qquad \left(\begin{array}{c} CONTEXTUALIZED \\ ABILITIES \end{array} \right)$$

Productivity demonstrates the amount of time and effort required to yield specific results.	Experience highlights work elements that facilitate or interfere with the potential of productivity.	Effectiveness captures the current situation and identifies areas of improvement and experimentation opportunities.

Credit: C. Murray, 2019

Employee perception of their work experiences is a powerful and integral aspect of assessing effectiveness. In conjunction with more linear and traditional productivity metrics, experience assessments help contextualize quantitative measurements and offer more insight into what reality looks like and what changes are practical and impactful. When framed around work enablement—not feelings or preferences—employee perception provides real-time insight into whether people have what they need to focus, collaborate, and deliver. By identifying and eliminating friction, such as digital distractions from email or messaging platforms, clunky tools, unclear expectations, or misaligned workflows, leaders gain a clearer picture of what enables or obstructs effective work. This broader lens helps leaders to invest in the right systems, rituals, and relationships that connect people to their work and one another. The result is a positive-sum dynamic where employee well-being, performance, and business outcomes all improve.

Shifting to measure effectiveness requires companies to redesign their approach to Employee Experience and prioritize what enables quality work, rather than offering the nice-to-haves delivered through perks, events, or swag—"cultural confetti." These elements matter, but they cannot compensate for broken systems or unsupported teams. Instead, organizations must build a foundation of experience that supports high-quality work at the core. When companies strive to make every environment, tool, and interaction valuable to their employees and their responsibilities, they affirm that employee time and energy are worth investing in for the sake of the business. That shift creates a culture where performance is not only expected, but also enabled.

• •

Overall, modern work is at a turning point. For knowledge work to thrive in the future, companies must move beyond outdated productivity models and invest in what enables effectiveness. Systems that reduce friction, support cognition, and honor the human energy behind the work become integral to every company's holistic workplace strategy, facilitating meaningful change.

4

Mindsets for Change

Principles of Transformative Action

Transforming how work happens requires new tools and new mindsets. Executive leadership, frontline engagement, and trust building must evolve together to meet the realities of modern work. Organizational change does not succeed without executive leadership, as the phrase "Change starts at the top" states. However, the change that starts at the top is less about action plans and more about mindset and the capacity for embracing the unknown.

Sustained transformation requires treating change as a continuous dialogue—an ongoing recalibration driven by evolving conditions, priorities, and choices. Executives who meet this reality with flexibility and curiosity can unlock the creativity and problem-solving capacity that often lies dormant within their organizations.

Most companies face a formidable challenge in today's work environment and broader culture. The cause is a combination of stubborn, ingrained organizational habits and maladaptations from the era of the Great WFH Experiment, and the growing mistrust of big businesses in the years since *(Economic Policy Institute, Sojourner, and Reich 2025)*. In addition, humans are inherently adaptable, but, by nature, resistant to change that they do not initiate themselves. When change arrives suddenly, inertia occurs because the process wants to move faster than the people are able. For people to willingly and confidently move toward change, they need access to knowledge that shifts their mindset toward curiosity and adaptability. Research from McKinsey demonstrates that employees in organizations that enable them to be adaptable and offer resilience amid uncertainty are three times more innovative than their unsupported peers *(McKinsey 2024)*.

Share of employees who reported high innovative behavior,[1] %

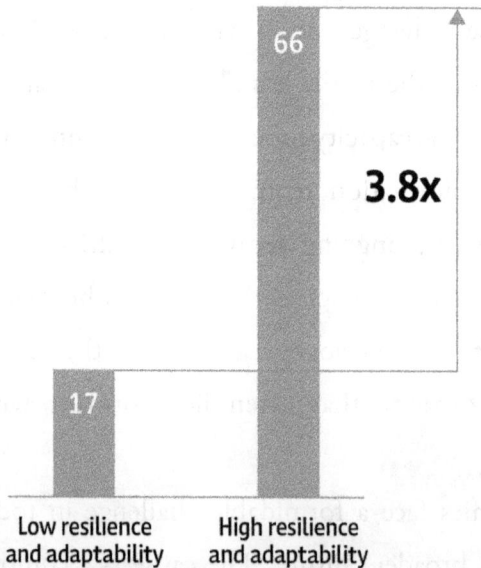

[1] Researchers sought responses to 3 statements about innovative behaviors. The statements were rated along a 5-point scale, from never (1) to very often (5). A high score was represented by those who, on average, reported positively to all the statements (≥). A low score was represented by all other responses (<4). Figures do not sum to total, because of rounding.

Source: McKinsey Health Institute survey of 30,000 employees in companies across 30 countries.

The foundation of adaptability and resilience starts with shifting how people metabolize and integrate change into their day-to-day work. Creating safe environments to experiment in and embracing new behaviors are the first steps toward major change.

Change as a Core Competency

McKinsey reports that 83 percent of leaders in high-growth companies actively encourage teams to test new ideas, fail quickly, and learn from the results *(McKinsey 2025)*. The core principles of dynamic work practices, like Lean Start-up, Holacracy, and Agile, are now table stakes for organizational survival in the twenty-first century. Although the necessity has continued to grow, the need for iteration and experimentation is not new. As Harvard Business Review put it in 2017: "All management is change management" *(Schaffer 2017)*. The message is clear: Business-as-usual is no longer viable. To lead well, you must expect and design for continuous change. Imagine how your leadership would shift if you prioritized ongoing adaptability over maintaining the status quo.

When companies approach transformation as a continuum, rather than a linear project with a beginning, middle, and end, they create a baseline of readiness for any challenge. Modern work demands this shift, which requires letting go of outdated attachments to certainty and control of outcomes. In their place, organizations must cultivate adaptability, resourcefulness, and resilience. These capabilities aren't just relevant in times of disruption, but essential for long-term success.

Rooting into New Leadership Mindsets

During organizational transformation, the greatest burden of behavioral change often falls on employees. Executives, by contrast, are rarely held to the same standard—an imbalance that reinforces the "us vs. them" divide, fuels mistrust, and undermines implementation. Modern work leaders must do more than sponsor change from above. They must engage with it themselves and adjust their behaviors in step with the shifts happening across the organization.

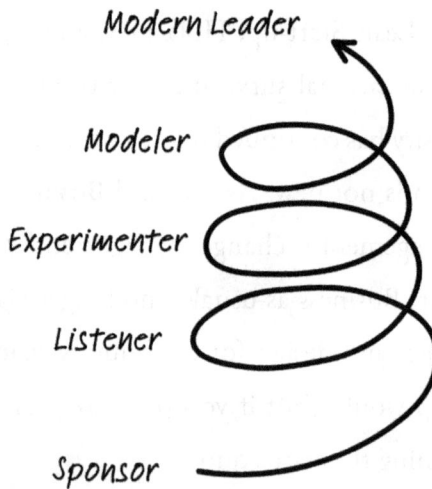

Modern Leader

Modeler

Experimenter

Listener

Sponsor

As the need for dynamic change within organizations increases in importance, Klaus Schwab's reflections on the Fourth Industrial Revolution and the Age of AI encapsulate the unique challenge that leaders must confront:

> The changes [brought by the Fourth Industrial
> Revolution] are so profound that, from the perspec-
> tive of human history, there has never been a time of

greater promise or potential peril. My concern, however, is that decision-makers are too often caught in traditional, linear (and non-disruptive) thinking or too absorbed by immediate concerns to think strategically about the forces of disruption and innovation shaping our future *(Schwab 2017)*.

Most executives are used to leading change within their sphere of control, relying on familiar tools, timelines, and confidence in the outcomes. However, the changes reshaping modern work defy these patterns; they are nonlinear, behavioral, and often beyond immediate comprehension or control. They require a different posture—one that values curiosity over certainty, iteration over prescription, and flexibility over fixed plans.

Leading modern transformation isn't about having the perfect blueprint; it's about creating the conditions for continuous adaptation.

For executives, that means moving beyond sponsorship toward participation by stepping into ambiguity, testing new models, and modeling responsiveness as a form of strategic strength. UC Berkeley psychologist Alison Gopnik explores this tension between structure and flow in her book, *The Gardener and The Carpenter*. Although originally intended for parenting, the framework applies just as powerfully to modern leadership. On one end of the spectrum is the carpenter, who values control, precision, and predetermined outcomes, shaping success like a crafted object. On the other hand, the gardener focuses on the environment, inputs, and adaptive care, creating the conditions for growth without dictating the result *(Gopnik 2016)*. Carpenters create stability through policies, programs, and infrastructure while gardeners nurture possibility by tuning into context and fostering resilience. The trouble comes when one dominates at the expense of the other.

CARPENTER   **GARDENER**

$\longleftrightarrow$

control, precision, predictability, structure   *adaptability, iteration, responsiveness, flow*

The challenges of modern work, and those we are likely to confront in the future, do not follow the blueprints we are familiar with. Thus, we must treat them as ecosystems that require tending by identifying the patterns that emerge and adapting accordingly. Change is no longer a series of discrete, predictable initiatives; it's a constant, evolving presence. Like invasive species that choke out growth in a garden, change can become unmanageable when we neglect its dynamic, shapeshifting nature. Despite this, many leaders still default to the carpenter mode: build from precedent, optimize for control, and seek protection from uncertainty.

Although unpredictability feels daunting to so many, it isn't a bug of modern work; it's a feature. In this model, antifragility becomes a leadership imperative. As Nassim Nicholas Taleb defines it, antifragile systems grow stronger under stress. When something is antifragile, it is strengthened and bolstered by disruption and change *(Taleb 2014)*.

FRAGILE

RESILIENT

ANTIFRAGILE

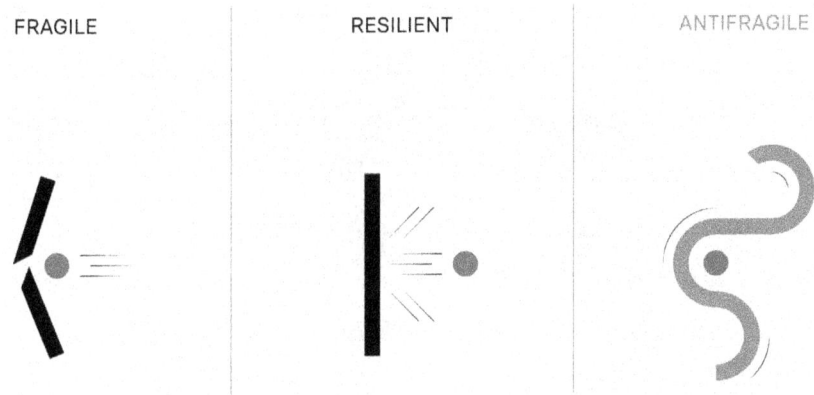

Credit to: Tatiana Barletta

Unlike resilient systems, which are sturdy enough to withstand uncertainty and volatility, antifragile systems are fortified and nimble in the face of future change. When setbacks occur, gardeners don't waste time rebuilding the same plan each time something changes. They acclimate, iterate, and learn. When shocks are beyond what carpenters can manage, the only path forward is to start from scratch again.

Importantly, this isn't a binary choice. Great leaders and organizations integrate both the craft of the carpenter, which gives shape to organizational structures, and the gardener, which gives companies the fluidity and adaptability needed in times of volatility. Embracing these two archetypes to shift leadership mindsets creates the conditions for broader engagement, but transformation doesn't scale without distributed advocates.

Change Champions 2.0

In traditional change management models, Change Champions are designated employees responsible for relaying information between executive teams and frontline staff. They are selected for their credibility, influence, and relatability among peers and across the organization. Ideally, they help translate broad strategy into localized action. In practice, however, many of these representatives serve as message carriers, tasked with transmitting one-way information from executives while bearing the brunt of employee frustrations, confusion, and resistance. Global benchmarking data shows that establishing formal Change Champion networks increases project success rates by nearly ten points *(Prosci 2024)*.

Despite their usual role in transformation, Change Champions can do so much more if given the agency and authority they deserve. Change Champions form the connective tissue between strategy and execution *(Prosci 2024)*. Change Champions are also rich sources of insight into how their area of the business operates and what is needed to drive greater success for both employees and the company. In this way, they provide real-time insights into how new policies and plans impact employee effectiveness. What's more, Change Champions understand the interdependencies within their functions, can anticipate resistance points, and often recognize what's needed for both people and processes to succeed. Despite this, Change Champions are typically underutilized in transformations or introduced into the transformation process too late for their insights to be integrated into the broader strategy. Typically, their bandwidth is limited, their authority constrained, and their insights often underleveraged.

At their best, Change Champions are empowered to act as interpreters, advocates, and adaptive agents. When employees are empowered to lead change from the bottom up, transformation success rates can rise over 70 percent *(McKinsey 2023)*. They help others connect the dots between executive vision and operational reality, building trust while resolving friction. They are the organizational sense-makers, translating context into relevance and responding with care when systems falter or sentiments shift.

Outside of large-scale transformations, few companies maintain an ongoing network of Change Champions. Instead, each new initiative tends to rebuild the network from scratch, missing the opportunity to retain and deepen institutional knowledge. In modern work, the downtime between transformation efforts has all but disappeared. As a result, this new rhythm of change demands a reimagined Change Champion model.

Some organizations may choose to formalize Change Champion roles as permanent fixtures of transformation or business enablement teams. Others might opt to establish ongoing Change Champion networks that flex across initiatives while staying anchored to long-term goals. Regardless of structure, the goal is the same: Build adaptive capacity into the business by embedding change as a shared competency. In this way, when Change Champions evolve from emissaries to embedded allies, change stops being imposed and starts becoming sustained. Change Champions help translate intent into practice, but that practice can't take hold without one critical ingredient: trust.

Demonstrate Trust to Earn It in Return

In our increasingly dynamic and disruptive business landscape, navigating change successfully requires deep organizational trust. While lateral trust across teams is essential for cross-functional collaboration and accomplishing business goals, lasting transformation depends on something more intrinsic: mutual trust between leaders and the workforce. Without it, even the most well-designed initiatives risk stalling.

Currently, many companies struggle to evolve and change due to a lack of reciprocal trust between organizations and their employees. The 2025 Edelman Trust Barometer revealed that, globally, 75 percent of employees do not trust their leaders and organizations to do what is right, a further decline from similar surveys in recent years *(Edelman 2025; Accenture et al. 2022)*. That's because employees often feel unseen or unheard, and leaders struggle to understand how work is done and what success looks like. What's more, when operating without that clarity, leaders frequently revert to control-based leadership practices, which reinforces a lack of trust and further disengages the workforce. To break this cycle, companies must stop treating trust as a matter of individual disposition and start designing for it at the systems level.

Trust, like culture, cannot be mandated. It must be modeled, measured, and maintained. Leadership listening is a powerful starting point. Research indicates that companies in the top percentiles for listening also rank in the eighty-eighth percentile for trust, while those at the bottom of the listening scale fall to only the thirteenth percentile for trust *(Zenger Folkman 2022)*. Trust and listening are mutually reinforcing—when leaders listen with intention, employees are more likely to speak up, share insights, and engage in change.

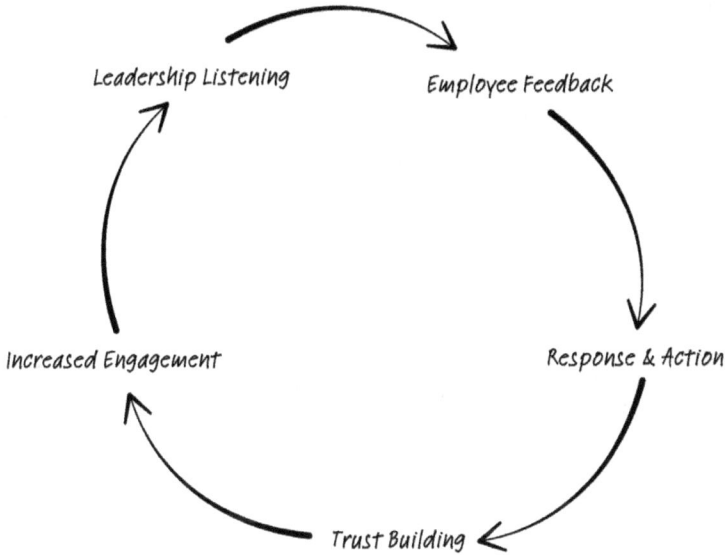

Leadership Listening

Employee Feedback

Increased Engagement

Response & Action

Trust Building

Systemic trust building means implementing visible, repeatable behaviors that signal psychological safety, accountability, and shared ownership. Over the past decade, terms such as "psychological safety" and "empathetic leadership" have gained increasing mainstream recognition. However, awareness of these concepts isn't enough. Companies must translate these values into systems and behaviors that shape daily interactions and provide foundational support for their employees.

Leading through change in this modern era of work doesn't require having all the answers. It requires cultivating the systems, behaviors, and relationships that allow better answers to emerge. Organizations that adapt to the dynamic conditions of business today recognize the need for antifragility and adaptability as we confront the accelerated changes of the Fourth Industrial Revolution.

5

Infrastructure
for Lasting Change
Sustainable Systems & Processes

Mindset shifts within your organization are crucial as the first step. However, without implementing updates to how your business operates, changes in perspective and attitude can become empty platitudes, leading to workforce frustration, disengagement, and a significant risk to business performance.

Mise en place is a French cooking methodology that translates to "everything in its place." It calls for all ingredients to be measured, prepared, and organized before beginning any recipe. Once the cooking process begins, your sole focus should be on incorporating the pre-set ingredients at the right time. Transformations in their own right, cooking and baking are most successful when all the pieces are laid out and ready to be incorporated when the time comes. That's because dividing your attention between chopping, measuring, stirring, and anything else can affect the quality and success of the dish.

Similarly, when it comes to organizational transformation, setting up systems to enable and sustain change while simultaneously managing transformation can undermine the success of both efforts. For transformations to be effective, the supporting infrastructure must be in place beforehand. Fortunately, most companies already have the necessary infrastructure, which simply needs to be repositioned or reconfigured to meet the new requirements. Before embarking on a workplace transformation, your company must complete a series of prerequisite exercises that allow behavior, workflow, policy, cultural norms, and overall systems to integrate effectively into the business, laying the groundwork for future opportunities and success.

Integrating Employee Feedback into Business Operations

Viewing Employee Experience solely through the lens of hospitality and customer service undermines the vital role employees play within their organizations. Incorporating employee feedback about the workplace and their work experiences is crucial to how organizations engage with their employees, which in turn affects the success of the business.

Incorporating employee feedback into your company's data ecosystem adds depth to the quantitative data that many companies currently rely on exclusively. It highlights the need for more frequent and targeted interactions with employees, moving beyond generic net promoter surveys. A 2024 Society for Human Resources Management (SHRM) study confirms that shifting feedback cycles from periodic to operational, real-time, and low-friction inputs allows leaders to make decisions immediately, while also acknowledging the competence and expertise of their workforce to enhance operations and the overall business *(SHRM Labs 2024)*.

This feedback can also facilitate the expansion of Change Champions' roles and responsibilities into an ongoing position of business advocacy and cross-collaboration. As trusted members of their respective teams, Change Champions can contextualize individual employee experiences within the broader organizational framework and identify practical and meaningful changes to improve current practices.

Although incorporating employee feedback into the cross-functional dynamics of the organization requires companies to operate with greater transparency and clarity, it does not necessitate that all information be equally accessible across the organization. This symbiotic feedback relationship entails regularly and broadly sharing essential information that impacts every employee's day-to-day work. Employees should not be caught off guard by changes; rather, these changes should be the welcome results of their expert input and feedback.

Cultivating Your Data

Every company generates a vast amount of data across tools, systems, and functions, but most of it lives in silos. As a result, executives often rely on intuition, historical precedent, or localized metrics that don't reflect the full organizational picture. Relying on gut instinct or outdated dashboards limits adaptability and amplifies bias. In a world defined by rapid and complex change, organizations can't afford to guess. Even well-meaning decisions can miss the mark when they're based on incomplete insight.

Establishing a holistic, interconnected view of your company's data and how it all coexists is the next step in continuing your company's digital transformation journey. Companies that unify their data can grow 19 percent faster and record 15 percent more profit than their competitors *(Forrester and Harrell 2020)*. Similarly, holistic, integrated data systems can double the effectiveness and reliability of insights and quadruple the speed at which teams can take action to make improvements and informed changes *(McKinsey et al. 2019)*. Yet without integration, blind spots proliferate. Disconnected systems obscure real conditions, expose organizations to risk, and complicate transformation efforts. Critical areas, such as Employee Experience, productivity, and enablement, suffer when no one has a complete view of the landscape.

Cultivating data is a two-pronged effort. First, connect disparate data sets to create a wider, more actionable vantage point. Second, equip decision-makers with the data literacy to interpret those insights and apply them wisely, which is especially vital when executives are several layers removed from day-to-day workflows. Their distance can enable perspective, but it can also breed data illiteracy if not deliberately bridged.

A cohesive, interconnected data ecosystem—where platforms speak to one another and tell a coherent story—offers a more resilient alternative. Instead of reinventing the wheel, focus on surfacing and connecting the systems already in place, identifying their points of connection, and forging shared meaning between interdependent teams that run them. The goal is not just to collect or generate more data, but to hone clearer narratives that reflect evolving, evidence-based understandings of how work is happening, what works, and where intervention is needed.

Data Coherence with The Daisy

If your company needs a starting point for linking data into a cohesive workplace narrative, we invite you to linger in the garden metaphor just a bit longer. The daisy has long symbolized new beginnings, and, in our context, it serves as a visual and strategic model for integrated workplace thinking.

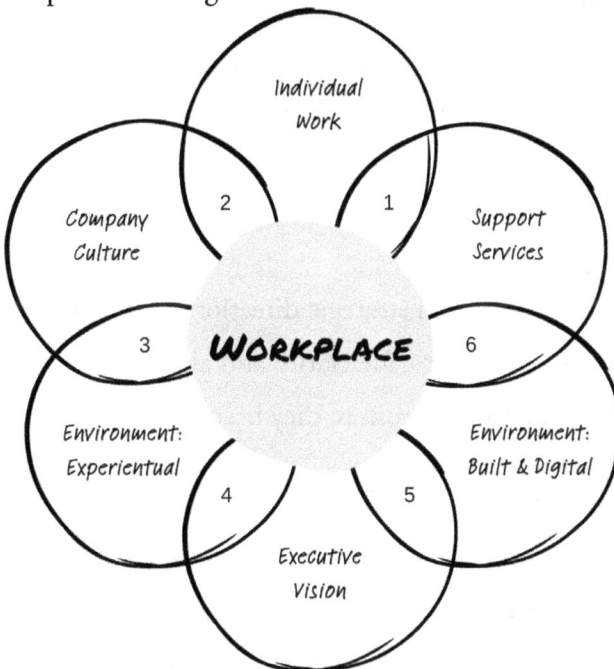

Credit: S. Escobar, 2016

This Workplace Daisy organizes data company-wide to support successful employees and businesses through the physical, digital, and experiential aspects of the workplace. If your company's enablement functions still operate in silos, organizing them through The Daisy's interdependent flow may help disparate business functions easily conceptualize how interdependent their work is and its role in facilitating effectiveness within the company.

The Daisy is a practical tool for surfacing how workplace decisions are made, who owns what, and where breakdowns—or breakthroughs—tend to occur. It reinforces that no function is isolated, and no workplace change can succeed without cross-functional coordination.

Individual Work

Employees' daily tasks, responsibilities, and workflows are where strategy meets reality, and it is here that breakdowns in enablement, clarity, or tools become most visible.

Executive Vision

The long-term goals and strategic direction of the company. When well-articulated, they provide clarity and alignment. When disconnected from day-to-day realities, they become abstractions.

Company Culture

The social and behavioral norms that guide how people work together. It either supports change or resists it, and is often revealed through employee actions more than intentions.

People Operations + HR (Experiential Environment)

The human side of the business; responsible for aligning talent development, policy, and well-being with broader business goals.

Internal Communications (Experiential Environment)

How and when information is shared within the organization. Often serves as a bellwether of a company's culture and how people perceive work, leadership, and change.

Real Estate & Facilities (Physical Environment)

The physical and most visible manifestation of the workplace. Cost-intensive and draws significant executive attention when considering the workplace, even though it's only one part of the larger picture.

IT + Tech (Digital Environment)

Owners of the digital environment and tools that employees rely on to do their jobs. Their reach is vast, but they're often disconnected from discussions about culture, space, or experience.

Support Services

The behind-the-scenes teams that maintain critical operations, facilities, and logistics.

The overlapping petals of The Daisy demonstrate the immediate impact of the interdependent relationships between enablement teams, leadership, and data within your organization:

1. Support services enable individual work, keeping their tools and resources functioning as expected.

2. The success and effectiveness of individual work exemplify the company culture, not the other way around.

3. This culture is documented and managed by the HR and Internal Communications teams.

4. However, whatever the HR and Internal Communications teams create transforms executive vision into policies and programs.

5. Real Estate and IT manage the digital and physical workplaces and most clearly facilitate the day-to-day work of individuals and teams.

6. However, without proper maintenance and support services, the physical and digital environments become outdated, and the promise of the workplace fails to deliver for employees and the organization.

In this way, The Daisy helps leaders map these dynamics, making it easier to see why certain investments fall flat or why some cultural goals fail to take root. When companies invest in strengthening the connections between petals, they move from fragmented fixes to system-level transformation.

Holistic, ongoing data flows that inform progress and improvements are essential for a workplace strategy to flourish. It's not just about square footage or survey scores. It's about designing for an ongoing flow of information, trust, decision-making, and accountability. When those elements are cultivated intentionally, The Daisy becomes a virtuous cycle that generates resilience, insight, and sustained adaptability in the workplace and organization.

Designing for Incremental Progress

In the 2018 book *Atomic Habits,* James Clear offers a low-friction, low-stakes approach to personal development and self-help. He suggests making minute changes that compound over time for lasting value. Clear begins by identifying five common pitfalls that derail even the most motivated efforts toward change, along with their simple antidotes.

Problem	Solution
Trying to change everything at once	Choose one thing, and do it well.
Starting with a change that's too big	Make the change so easy and appealing that you can't say no.
Seeking a result, not a ritual	Focus on the behavior, not the outcome.
Not changing your environment	Build an environment that promotes good habits intuitively.
Assuming small things don't add up	Get 1 percent better every day.

(Clear 2018)

Shifting our approach and expectations of change is what makes change easier. These individual challenges mirror—and often intensify—organizational life. As a result, many workplace transformations fall prey to the same pitfalls: trying to overhaul everything at once, chasing results without changing behavior, and undervaluing incremental progress.

One adage remains true: Meaningful change takes time. Learning, adapting, and evolving require deliberate pacing. While the pressures of modern business may demand speed, sustainable transformation favors depth over haste. Documenting incremental progress is essential. As described earlier, frameworks like The Daisy depend on tracking incremental changes across roles and systems, making it easier to identify which actions support both workforce needs and business goals.

Organizational Outputs

Work outputs measure effectiveness and directly inform a business's revenue, profitability, valuation, and other key metrics. These outputs can vary based on the role, location, company, and other factors, but often include all or a portion of the following:

Deliverables

The tangible work produced by individuals or teams that drives business results.

Relationships

Partnerships, trust networks, and shared understanding make

collaboration possible and scalable. These relationships span people, tools, culture, and norms, and together form the infrastructure of a healthy organization.

Transformation

The forward motion that keeps organizations competitive requires executive vision and employee insight to identify and understand operational pain points and can co-design solutions.

Retention

Experience and insight are often lost when employees leave an organization. Retention refers to the process of keeping both individuals and the knowledge they possess by supporting their need for growth, balance, and purpose, along with the safety of speaking up about what's not working.

All in all, a great workplace provides the inputs—tools, systems, and policies—that enable successful outputs.

Balancing External Shifts with Organizational Realities

Companies don't operate in a vacuum; they respond constantly to shifting economic, competitive, and social conditions. Executives rely on economists, strategists, and analysts to track these trends and assess how external factors, such as competitor behavior or market volatility, impact business risk and opportunity.

Yet, too often, workplace data is left out of this equation. In The Daisy framework, executive vision is deliberately not the first input into workplace strategy. It follows from understanding the actual work conditions and the organizational capacity for change. For example, many recent Return to Office mandates were not grounded in internal data that showed improved performance or engagement. They were based on executive preference and on watching what peers like JPMorgan or Amazon were doing. These decisions disregarded internal signals, including low office adoption, declining morale, and a limited impact on the bottom line.

This pattern isn't new. Workplace decisions often follow precedent more than insight, even when better data exists. But as pressure rises—from economic uncertainty, reputational risk, or workforce disengagement—companies that fail to integrate internal realities with external shifts pay the price. That's why executives who align external sensing with internal evidence make better decisions. It's because they can identify when trends apply to their context, and when change is needed, they're equipped to move early and clearly, avoiding the shocks and slowdowns that come with a reactive strategy.

Overall, the point is not to predict the future. But rather to build a system that makes your organization more adaptive when the future arrives. That means embedding key indicators—both internal and external—into daily operations so when the next disruption hits, you won't need to guess how to respond. You'll already know what your organization needs to stay grounded and move forward.

Organizing Leaders Around Company Data

Once data is interconnected, the first step is to take honest stock of your current state—what's working, what's failing, and what's simply unclear. Rather than reactive problem-solving, this type of systemic review enables organizations to address root causes and align their daily operations with their stated values.

Yet, this alignment won't happen unless leaders across the organization engage with data in a meaningful way. According to recent studies, two-thirds of executives still rely more on gut instinct than data, while 97 percent of data leaders report that ignoring insights has led to negative consequences. Lack of data is not the issue that companies struggle with; rather, it is the lack of urgency around data literacy and its role in decision-making *(Accenture and Qlik 2020; Alation and Wakefield Research 2021)*.

Understanding how data sets connect—and what those connections reveal—is now a foundational leadership skill. Today, over 85 percent of leaders in the US and UK recognize data literacy as an essential skill within their workforces. Despite this, 50 percent of them deal with a skills gap in this area. The Daisy provides both a wide-angle view and granular detail of a company's functional health, clarifying how each discipline contributes to and depends on the others. This shared accountability structure serves as a gateway to greater data literacy by helping teams identify patterns, surface issues, and act with confidence. In this way, The Daisy is both a diagnostic tool and a coordination mechanism—a way to bring together stakeholders across functions under a shared vision. Mapping relationships between disciplines reduces friction and turf battles, making it easier for leaders to collaborate rather than compete.

Organizations that adopt this shared framework build resilience into their transformation efforts. Instead of treating each initiative as a one-off project, they create conditions where change becomes embedded—and where leadership at every level contributes to collective progress. Leadership structures vary across companies, but for workplace transformation, three key groups emerge:

Executive Leaders

Responsible for enterprise-level strategy, growth, and long-term stability.

Business Leaders

Oversee the performance and alignment of specific functions or segments.

People Leaders

Manage individuals and teams, shaping the daily work experience.

Each plays a distinct role. Executives set the vision, business leaders translate that vision into operational strategy, and people leaders ensure that the strategy is supported, understood, and sustained in the day-to-day. The Daisy helps all three groups stay connected to the realities of the workforce.

Establishing clear leadership and data structures before initiating an organizational change ensures that actions taken are contextualized with the needs of employees and the business. Centralizing and visualizing data to help leaders from across your organization understand the role they and their work play in the broader scope of transformation creates buy-in and momentum needed for your workforce to feel supported through the changes to come.

6

Model Behavior

Theories & Approaches that Shaped Work then Place

The *WORK then PLACE* process was inspired by and lever-
ages insights from six models and approaches that represent the
unique needs of people experiencing change and transformation.
Throughout our careers, we've incorporated many of these processes
into the transformations we've led. Others, however, are included in
WORK then PLACE because of the lessons we've learned and the
gaps that many transformations still possess. They are:

- The Transtheoretical Model of Behavior Change
  (Prochaska and DiClemente 1977)

- The Stages of Grief *(Kübler-Ross 1969)*

- Mindset Shifts *(McKinsey, Basford, and Schaninger 2016)*

- Time Well Spent *(Norton and Pine 2009)*

- Too Long; Didn't Read *(TL;DR ~2002)*

The Transtheoretical Model of Behavior Change

The Transtheoretical Model of Behavior Change, developed by psychologists James Prochaska and Carlo DiClemente in 1977, reminds us that change is not linear, and relapse and recovery are possible at any stage of the process. This model outlines a sequence of psychological stages that individuals typically oscillate between, each with distinct needs and barriers. Understanding these stages and the likely causes for breakdowns and failures that occur helps transformation teams meet people where they are, not just where the organization wants them to be.

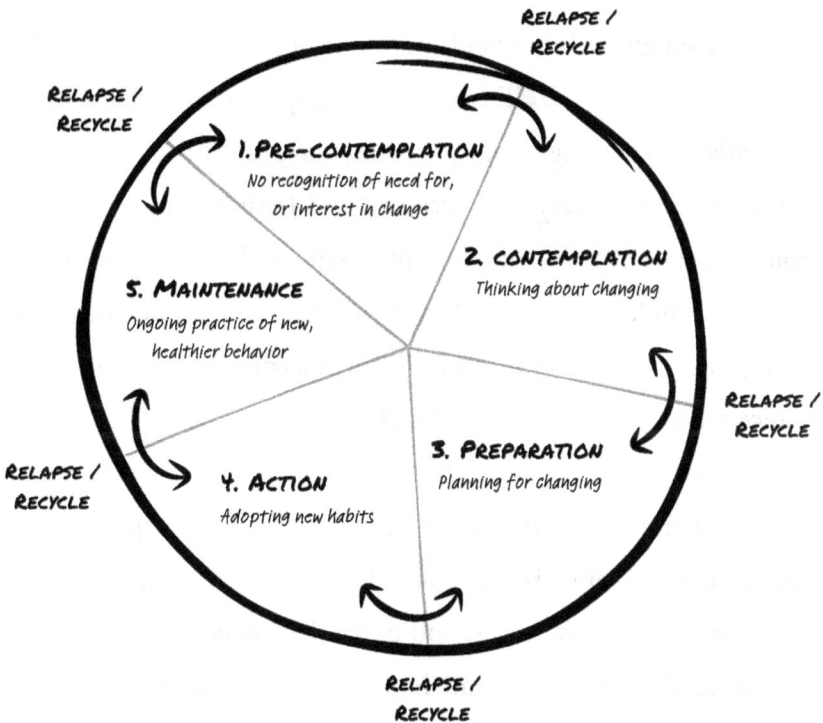

RELAPSE / RECYCLE

RELAPSE / RECYCLE

1. PRE-CONTEMPLATION
No recognition of need for, or interest in change

2. CONTEMPLATION
Thinking about changing

5. MAINTENANCE
Ongoing practice of new, healthier behavior

RELAPSE / RECYCLE

3. PREPARATION
Planning for changing

RELAPSE / RECYCLE

4. ACTION
Adopting new habits

RELAPSE / RECYCLE

Many failed change efforts stall in the early phases—Precontemplation, Contemplation, and Preparation—before any real action begins. In Precontemplation, people may not even recognize a need for change. Even with compelling communication, it can feel like inertia or even resistance when change activities are out of sync with organizational readiness. In Contemplation, individuals start to weigh the pros and cons of change, but doubt, fear, or confusion often delay momentum. This phase requires clarity and reassurance as people begin to imagine what change looks like for them. When people are preparing, they need the right structures, encouragement, and timing to help them feel ready to take the leap. If reinforcement feels too rigid or is not firm enough, readiness fades.

WORK then PLACE treats these early phases as the scaffolding—steps, tools, language, and pacing—to guide people into active participation necessary for successful and lasting change. Creating holistic data networks, shifting mindsets, and understanding the unique complexities of modern work generate groundswells for change, helping teams approach change as a conscious and confident choice rather than an organizational mandate.

Critically, each person's reaction to change is shaped by their history, identity, and position in the company. This emphasizes the importance for organizations and leaders to understand generational differences, life stages, and psychological context. By tuning into these differences, we can shape transformation plans that are both more human and more effective.

The goal isn't to move people through a predetermined change funnel, but to build a culture of trust and readiness where change is welcomed instead of feared. When change gets messy—as it always does—these same principles help teams course-correct and move forward again.

The Stages of Grief

Replacing old and outdated behaviors with new, relevant ones is a challenging process. Assuming that transformation follows a single, progressive path makes the journey even more difficult. *Stages of Grief* by Elisabeth Kübler-Ross is frequently used as a foundation for human-centered change management because it acknowledges the disruption of perceived loss and the accompanying grief that many face.

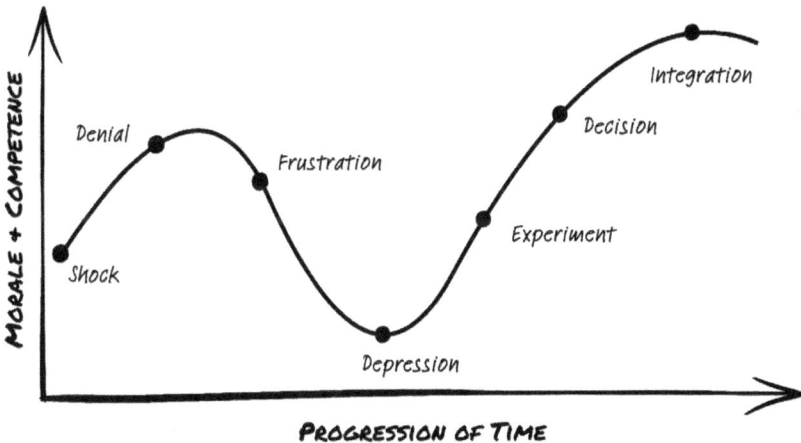

When examining human-centered change management in relation to the Transtheoretical Model of Behavior Change (TMBC), it is crucial to understand the distinction between resistance and relapse behaviors. Resistance to change—reflecting a conscious pushback against change and what it represents—is natural and can be worked through with deeper interventions and partnership. On the other hand, relapse is more representative of the inability to internalize change or readjust to new circumstances, which requires a reevaluation or redesign of approaches to pursue approaches that are more compatible with practical realities.

TMBC focuses on the behaviors associated with each phase of change, and the Kübler-Ross Change Curve (KRCC) acknowledges the emotional peaks and valleys that accompany change. The two models complement one another, addressing different aspects of how people experience change and informing what kind of actions might be necessary to ease them through each phase without creating resistance or relapse.

TMBC	KRCC	Common Characteristics
Precontemplation	Shock, Denial	Ignorance or lack of awareness of change efforts or the need for them
Contemplation	Frustration, Depression	Emergence of awareness that change cannot be avoided
Preparation	Experimentation	Efforts that begin to bridge the gap between the proposed future and reality
Action	Decision-Making	Learning and implementing of agreed-upon, future-state behaviors
Maintenance	Integration	Arrival at the future state when a new baseline is established

These indicators help identify influences that may impact progress to the next stage of behavioral change by shifting the mindset of co-creators. The *WORK then PLACE* process is designed around several cycles of change and mindset shifts, emphasizing that one round of change is just the beginning of a new cycle of learning and iteration.

Mindset Shifts

Change is a complex process that requires not only time and patience but also careful planning, courage, and, most critically, a willingness to try new things. The *WORK then PLACE* framework emphasizes a culture of experimentation, continuous learning, and the integration of new practices. McKinsey's Influence Model complements the TMBC and KRCC frameworks by focusing on the individual needs that must be met for change to be successfully adopted at each stage of a transformation. Creating encouragement, inspiration, and practical applications for how and where changes fit into daily life makes change feel like a natural evolution rather than a disruptive force in an organization.

> ## I WILL CHANGE MY MINDSET AND BEHAVIOR IF AND WHEN...
>
> **Role Modeling**
> "I notice leaders, colleagues, and staff behaving differently."
>
> **Developing Talent & Skills**
> "I have access to what I need to help me adopt a new approach."
>
> **Fostering Understanding & Conviction**
> "I know what change is asked of me and why it's important ."
>
> **Reinforcing with Formal Mechanism**
> "I see structures, processes, and systems support the changes."

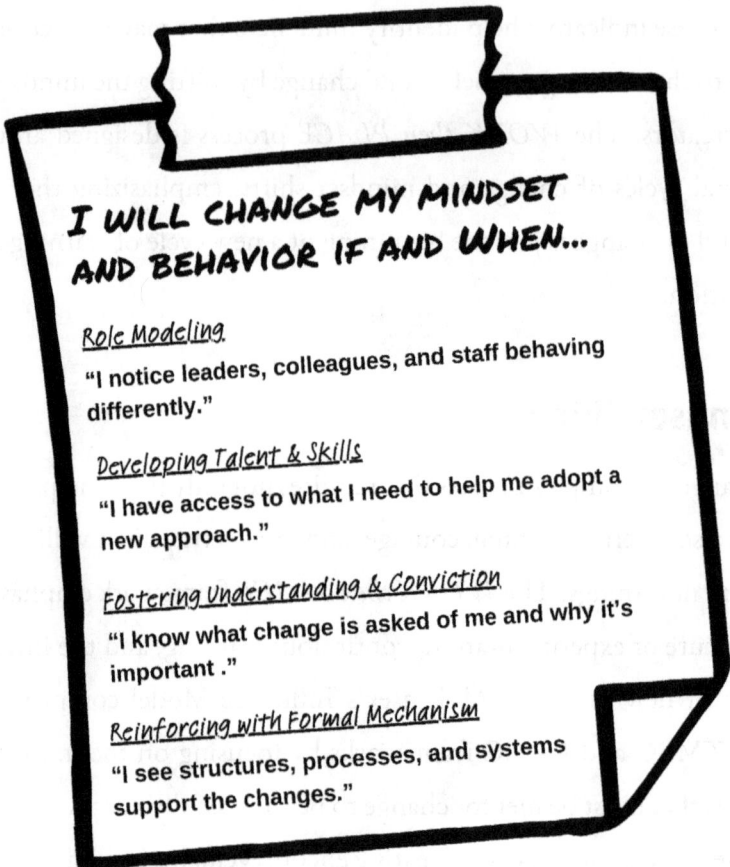

This model identifies four areas that facilitate change through organizational influence:

Role Modeling

People are inclined to imitate the behaviors and actions of those around them, both on a conscious level through deliberate observation and on an unconscious level through social cues. This means that leaders and peers play a vital role in shaping the behavior of others within the organization.

Fostering Understanding and Conviction

Individuals are more likely to commit to change when they perceive a clear alignment between their personal beliefs and the behaviors expected of them. Understanding the underlying rationale, or the *why*, behind a change fosters a sense of ownership and promotes supportive behaviors.

Developing Skills and Talent

Contrary to the belief that old habits are hard to break, research on neuroplasticity suggests that our neural pathways can be continually reshaped and reformed. When well supported and contextualized, upskilling and professional growth can lead to greater individual and organizational effectiveness.

Reinforcing with Formal Mechanisms

Behaviors are influenced by surroundings, which is why broadening the definition of the workplace to encompass the digital and experiential ecosystems, in addition to the physical ecosystem, is so essential. When organizations fail to establish a cohesive workplace strategy, they unintentionally reinforce or encourage behaviors that don't support their goals and objectives.

These strategies, when paired with the TMBC and KRCC frameworks, emphasize the importance of seeing, hearing, discussing, experiencing, and teaching at each stage. The influence model provides clear objectives and attributed tasks that help garner motivation and enthusiasm for change at each stage of a broader transformation.

Time Well Spent

Similar to design-thinking principles like "keep, toss, create," and "rose, bud, thorn," the Time Well Spent framework is designed to uncover the types of experiences that are valuable and to whom, as well as to identify opportunities for innovation and improvement.

Introduced by Dave Norton and Joe Pine in 2009, this framework was initially focused on understanding what shapes consumer behaviors and how brands could reposition their offerings and approaches to create customer loyalty and corresponding revenue gains. Time Well Spent offers a versatile approach that concentrates on employee feedback and provides organizations with actionable insights.

The framework is divided into four distinct categories:

Time Wasted

When experiences fall short of expectations or fail to deliver value. Some examples include extractive, disjointed, or unnecessary interactions that leave people frustrated or disengaged.

Time Well Saved

When efficiencies reduce friction and free up cognitive or calendar space. Streamlined processes, intuitive tools, and clear communication that lighten the load, freeing up valuable time for people to reinvest elsewhere.

Time Well Spent

When experiences feel meaningful, reciprocal, and energizing. They are marked by purpose, quality interaction, and alignment with personal or professional values.

Time Well Invested

When initial effort yields an outsized, but delayed benefit. Learning, relationship-building, or foundational work all generate long-term payoff and momentum.

From the perspective of effectiveness, anything that disrupts the ability to produce quality work within a reasonable timeframe contributes to an organization's Time Wasted. The Time Well Spent methodology provides a framework for companies to align their operational processes with how work is performed.

TL;DR

The final element is not a model but rather an approach that is universally important in change and transformation: fostering understanding. If the people you are communicating with cannot understand your message, they will not be able to internalize it. The slang term "TL;DR," emerged in online forums and discussion boards in 2002 and has been widely adopted, especially by start-up companies. It emphasizes the importance of communicating in a clear and accessible manner. TL;DRs take a longer, more detailed version of an idea and condense it into the key points that should be retained as takeaways.

Documenting the context and background of a change—including relevant stories, background information, and key decision factors—is essential to any successful change initiative. Additionally, considering the most efficient means of delivering information is equally important, often meaning that the information needs to be streamlined into a style that is easy to understand and internalize. Similar to abstracts and summaries of reports, TL;DRs provide a concise set of key takeaways that people can refer back to as needed.

Even if you have established knowledge-sharing methodologies, TL;DRs are invaluable in the workplace and any change management process. Their foundation lies in conveying vital information in a clear and easy-to-absorb format. Those affected by workplace changes often do not see the challenges that organizations navigate in order to make and implement decisions. To successfully integrate change, it is essential to meet those affected where they are, regardless of their engagement in the broader process. They should not have to worry about navigating workplace complexities, as this is not their primary responsibility. TL;DRs help them grasp the story behind the change in a digestible manner, facilitating buy-in without taking significant time away from their core responsibilities.

Countless models and frameworks can help your company along its path of transformation, but as we created the *WORK then PLACE* process, these were the ones that rang most true for us. Specific theories and research can be interchanged based on your company's unique style and approach to change. However, the intention of implementing change that balances process with human behavior and thoroughness with brevity should always remain.

SECTION TWO:

W.O.R.K.

Changing mindsets and habits is the first—and most essential—step in any workplace transformation. Before physical environments can shift, organizations must establish how people work together, how decisions are made, and how norms are formed. The WORK section is where workplace transformation starts—not with the design of a new space, but with the design of new behaviors.

The WORK phase focuses on defining, piloting, and embedding behavioral change.

Across the next four chapters, we will:

- **Define** <u>W</u>hy change is needed and <u>W</u>hat to do about it.

- **Operationalize** the Why into practical, data-informed actions.

- **Regulate** outcomes to create new norms.

- Establish **Knowledge Bases**, the centralized sources of truth that keep everyone aligned and working toward common objectives.

These chapters offer a step-by-step approach to transforming behavior without overcomplicating it. Each one emphasizes clarity over control, learning over perfection. The goal is to move from theory to practice—to test, adjust, and refine behavior in ways that reduce friction, build trust, and make change durable.

What you learn in WORK directly informs PLACE. Norms must come first. Office layouts, events, and technology follow, not as culture drivers, but as culture enablers.

Each chapter closes with a case study drawn from our careers—real engagements that surfaced lessons, wins, and challenges. These stories give texture to the frameworks and reinforce a central idea: WORK precedes PLACE. Always.

7

What & Why

Clarifying Purpose Before Change

TL;DR

Every transformation needs a North Star—a clear, shared sense of purpose. Without it, even the best tools and strategies fall flat. Define what's changing, why it matters, and how it connects to what your company stands for. Alignment at this stage turns intention into action and builds momentum for everything that follows.

As the pace of change in the business world continues to accelerate, it is essential for organizations to clearly define and uphold their purpose, often referred to as their "North Star," and how the actions they take support the pursuit of it. Studies from McKinsey and MIT Sloan indicate that organizations with a clear and well-communicated purpose experience significantly higher productivity, engagement, and adaptability compared to those without one *(McKinsey et al. 2018)* *(MIT Sloan et al. 2022).*

W

NORTH STAR

OPERATING PRINCIPLES

WORKFLOWS / BEHAVIORS / NORMS

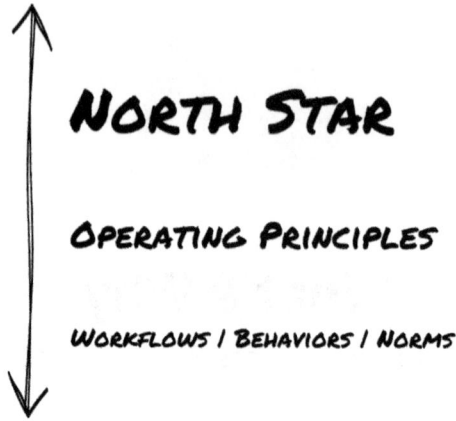

Leaders often talk about vision, but transformation needs more than slogans. A North Star defines success beyond metrics—it gives meaning and direction to the work that must be incorporated throughout all aspects of the change and revisited often.

Leaders must define principles that guide action, not just the intention of developing guiding principles that convey the tone and direction their organizations will follow. Operating with purpose is crucial for achieving success and remaining competitive in the broader business landscape. These prerequisites are universal and serve as the foundational building blocks that companies need to thrive in the twenty-first century.

For a company's What and Why to truly manifest, it must guide the direction of every project and initiative within the organization. Organizations that organize their teams around a common purpose are 2.4 times more likely to set a clear direction for the business *(McKinsey 2024)*. A common thread runs through these initiatives that fosters both strategic coherence and workforce stability.

Identifying your *WORK then PLACE* **What**

W

Establishing the What requires focusing on indicators that signal the need for change in the first place. Each change within a company, regardless of its scope or scale, must connect specific, targeted adjustments to the broader purpose that guides its operations and leadership decisions. Your *WORK then PLACE* What is most successful when it aligns with the organization's overarching North Star, the grand Why, and is compatible with its overall direction and purpose.

When every Workplace and Employee Experience initiative is anchored to your company's North Star, workforce and operational evolution can move in sync. The success and longevity of any *WORK then PLACE* process depends on this alignment. Data ecosystems, such as The Daisy, make this possible by enabling hierarchical decision-making, linking daily choices to strategic direction, and keeping purpose at the center.

Too often, an organization's purpose exists separately from its operational management. This disconnect creates a rift between executive intent and Employee Experience, leading to fragmented decisions about how, where, and why people work, often undermining the very direction companies aim to pursue.

Framing the Why Behind the What

When organizations consider how to facilitate quality work, they often focus on where work occurs rather than on why or how it

W should be done. This long-standing assumption regarding in-office work has persisted for many years. However, due to the unfolding events of the 2020s, this norm has recently been questioned and challenged within mainstream culture. Modern work requires us to determine where work can be done most effectively for different workers and work styles to achieve the best outcomes. To make this expansive task manageable, we should break these concepts into smaller, digestible pieces and tackle them step by step.

Consider an arena: People don't come for the building itself, they come for the experiences it makes possible. Behind the scenes, a robust technological infrastructure powers essential systems, including lighting, airflow, and security. High-capacity Wi-Fi supports both critical operations and the surge of personal devices. Hospitality services—food, beverages, merchandise, and branded gear—elevate the overall experience. But, above all, there must be a compelling reason to gather: the entertainment that gives the space its purpose.

Whether it's The Eras Tour, the WNBA Finals, or the World Series, people visit these arenas for specific reasons. However, there are now more ways than ever for individuals to engage with this type of entertainment, often requiring only a power source, an internet connection, and a screen. These alternatives fit more easily into day-to-day life. But when the objective is to create as many immersive experiences as possible for the same event and make them accessible to as many people as possible, the possibilities are endless.

Companies that recognize their responsibility to make success at work as accessible as watching a Beyoncé concert at NRG Stadium in Houston, broadcasting it, and then having it available for viewing on Netflix the next day will thrive. This approach benefits not only their customers, who are employees in this case, but also the business itself. When we recognize that the physical environment is only one aspect of a company's overall workplace, we quickly realize that digital ecosystems and organizational behaviors are the other two key components that create stable and successful work environments, propelling both workforces and their businesses forward.

With the insights gathered and aligned throughout The Daisy, the What aligns with the larger purpose and guiding principles your company is aiming for. This framework helps clarify what needs to be addressed within your organization. Whether you choose to focus on ease of implementation, urgency, or another factor to build your What, the information articulated in The Daisy will assist you in determining the best path to achieve your goals.

Pursuing Alignment & Calibrating Objectives

Once your purpose of change and initial steps are clearly defined, the first phase of engaging with your workforce begins. Your mission at this stage is to craft a compelling narrative that clearly communicates both the pilot objectives and the path to achieving them.

Clarity is essential to the process of fostering a true sense of unity. Draw on insights from The Daisy, the catalyst for change, and highlight the key themes that shaped your compelling Why. Aim for conciseness without losing critical details and craft a narrative

W

that connects executive ambitions with workforce needs and organizational realities, translating vision into tangible goals. Teams can maintain this alignment by focusing on the following objectives:

Iterative Prioritization

It's impractical to tackle every issue at once. Focus pilot efforts around transforming specific, targeted issues based on estimated impact, ease of implementation, and perceived urgency. Narrow your options and concentrate your efforts.

Multidirectional Partnership

Share preliminary concepts and the required resources with stakeholders, participants, and delivery partners, and refine assumptions based on their context and expertise. Building these relationships will help assess the viability of your ideas and identify opportunities for refining and adjusting your priorities.

Applied Empathy

Be prepared for initial concepts to evolve. Edits and enhancements are not signs of faulty ideas and concepts. Rather, they are a necessary part of the progression that ideas must undergo to develop into well-rounded strategies. Stay focused on why change is needed, but remain flexible regarding how that change might unfold.

Solidifying the Go-Forward

As teams advance through WORK then PLACE, confidence and perceived competence will fluctuate, a pattern explained by the Dunning-Kruger Effect. The only wrong choice is choosing a change that's too big or vague. If you're unsure if the change you and your team have selected is too big, consider the actions that come with it. Always aim to change the lowest common denominator, the challenge or challenges most recognizable and nameable by the largest number of people *(The New York Times and Ovide 2021)*.

W

Make sure to align and document the various adjustments and agreements made through this initial iterative exercise. Then, document each modification with commentary that explains the rationale behind the change and identifies the stakeholders involved in its approval. Share any adjustments made to the timeline, updates to role assignments, and the next steps required to maintain transparency and uphold accountability throughout the process.

Leading teams through *WORK then PLACE* often reveals the Dunning-Kruger curve in action. This concept describes how confidence can fluctuate as one gains knowledge and expertise.

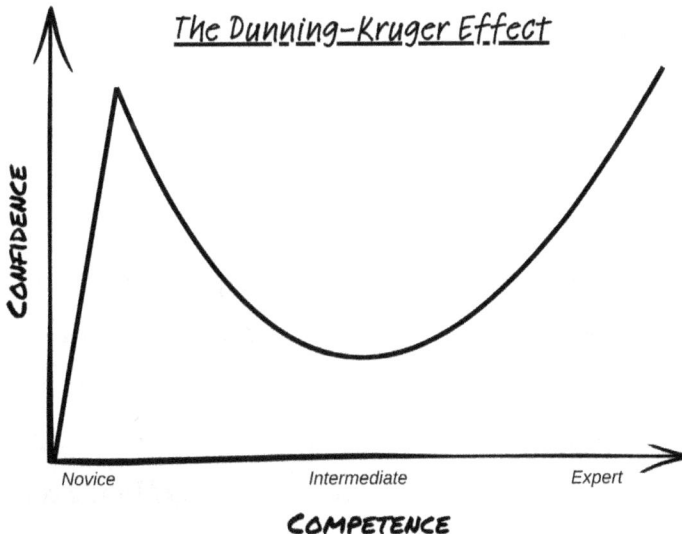

The Dunning-Kruger Effect

CONFIDENCE

Novice   Intermediate   Expert

COMPETENCE

W

Initially, confidence may soar even when competence is still below average, similar to a "honeymoon phase" where everything seems positive and essential realities are overlooked. However, as individuals gain more competence, confidence often plummets when they start to recognize and confront difficult truths. As the journey continues and competence improves to an average or above-average level, confidence and trust are gradually rebuilt, correlating with the development of expertise *(Dunning and Kruger 1999)*.

Those leading and supporting others through a *WORK then PLACE* transformation will likely experience just as much change, if not more, than those they are trying to help. Developing expertise often involves cycles of confidence and doubt that require patience with yourself and others as you continue to learn and accommodate. As you continue refining mindsets, methods, and strategies, remember that clarity of purpose also strengthens workplace antifragility. When individuals and teams understand the Why behind their work practices, they're better equipped to acclimate, improve, and thrive.

Measuring Success

Many organizations overcomplicate measurement, especially in non-technical settings. Although tools like spreadsheets and Tableau can yield insightful visualizations, poor data literacy at all levels of an organization remains a barrier. Simpler, clearer success metrics are often more effective than complex data models, especially when building a motivated coalition for change. In the context of experimentation, metrics should offer unambiguous guidance: Should we continue, pause, pivot, or stop? The most useful measures reveal the gap between the current state and desired outcomes, providing a grounded basis for evaluating progress and making informed decisions.

Framing, defining, and articulating What you aim to achieve with your partners makes success metrics more straightforward. Your organization should be clear about the outcomes it wants to achieve. After that, it becomes a matter of tracking progress and being willing to modify as lessons emerge. This process is easier with connected input systems, such as The Daisy, which help track how changes impact the overall Workplace Experience. It also becomes easier when employee feedback is treated with the same importance as customer feedback in the digital product life cycle.

Feedback from employees and other participants in the experiments should communicate which concepts are easy to implement, valuable to their work, and offer tangible improvements to their day-to-day experiences. Pairing this brief analysis with minimally invasive pulse survey cues for employees involved in the pilots can provide a week-to-week view of progress without requiring a full-scale research exercise, which could further delay progress and diminish employee motivation and momentum for change.

••

W

To illustrate the WORK process in action, we will use a continuous example throughout these process chapters focused on meetings and meeting culture, which is an aspect of work that almost universally requires improvement. Evolving a company's meeting culture can change organizational behaviors and Employee Experience. It also informs how a company's workplace must modify to meet the needs of a workforce and the organizational goals they work toward.

In Theory

The Meeting Dilemma: When Work Gets Stuck

Meeting rooms are among the most expensive and inefficient areas of the built environment on a per-square-foot basis. According to commercial real estate and investments firm CBRE, building physical meeting space can cost up to $554 per square foot *(CBRE Insights 2024)*. Companies that dedicate attention to auditing, evaluating, and evolving meeting behaviors not only create new opportunities for focus and creativity within their workforce but can also reap benefits that optimize workplace operations and reduce costs.

Leaders today face the ongoing challenge of guiding their companies to achieve more with fewer resources. This pressure extends to business leaders and the entire workforce. We all know that "time is zero sum," yet companies struggle to implement the necessary changes to reclaim time *(Perlow, Hadley, and Eun 2017)*. This difficulty often stems from organizational transformations that focus on business processes and policies without adopting improved practices for how work, particularly knowledge work, is conducted. The thesis that underpins the WORK then PLACE process is that behaviors must shape our environments rather than the other way around. The Ways of Working Matrix in Chapter 3 highlights the four essential aspects of knowledge work, and a workforce's ability to excel in these areas is crucial for a company's success in productivity, effectiveness, profitability, and other key metrics. And back to basics: One of the significant challenges employees face daily, which has serious implications for the organization as a whole, is the sheer volume of meetings they attend.

Addressing a company's meeting culture is a popular approach to tackling both operational challenges and the struggles employees experience. In many organizations, recurring meetings are often seen as a waste of time. The phrase "This meeting should have been an email" was common before 2020. Still, its relevance has surged since then, resulting in a variety of merchandise made in its honor on platforms such as Etsy, Amazon, and local boutiques across the United States.

In August 2017, Harvard Business Review published an article titled "Stop the Meeting Madness." In a related study of 182 senior managers across various industries, 65 percent reported

W

that meetings prevented them from completing their work, 71 percent deemed meetings unproductive and inefficient, 64 percent felt that meetings hindered deep thinking, and 62 percent stated that meetings missed opportunities to strengthen team cohesion. Unfortunately, since that study, the data surrounding meetings has only worsened *(Perlow, Hadley, and Eun 2017)*.

Between February 2020 and February 2022, the time spent in virtual meetings surged by 250 percent *(Pellegrini and Microsoft 2022)*. Although this staggering increase was largely due to all in-person meetings shifting to virtual formats during the COVID-19 pandemic, the behavior nonetheless became normalized. In the absence of the casual run-ins and catch-up conversations in the office, our calendars and virtual meeting rooms became the new location for everything, and our schedules became even more unforgiving. Despite most companies shifting to structured hybrid work policies, where people are in the office together for certain days each week, the behaviors have not recalibrated with the change of scenery.

On the individual level, Slack interviewed 10,000 workers from around the world and found that more than two hours of meetings per day—what they named the "Goldilocks Zone"—was the maximum amount of time employees could manage before it interfered with their ability to focus on their responsibilities and tasks *(Slack 2023)*. Similarly, a 2021 study by Microsoft found that back-to-back meetings can lead to a buildup of stress

Your brain works differently when you take breaks

Taking time out between video calls prevents stress from building up.

W

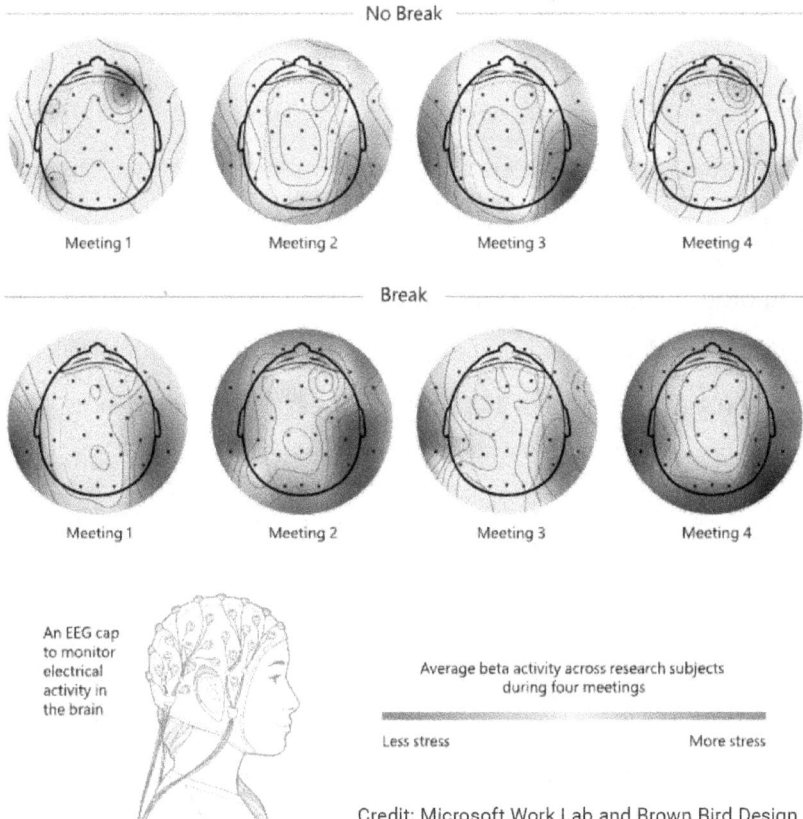

No Break

Meeting 1   Meeting 2   Meeting 3   Meeting 4

Break

Meeting 1   Meeting 2   Meeting 3   Meeting 4

An EEG cap to monitor electrical activity in the brain

Average beta activity across research subjects during four meetings

Less stress   More stress

Credit: Microsoft Work Lab and Brown Bird Design

in the brain, which increases the risk of errors and poor decision-making. The Yale Medical School research mentioned in Chapter 1 confirmed that the human brain processes in-person interactions more easily than virtual ones. Despite the evidence showing that the value of virtual meetings declines with each passing hour, they remain a staple in today's work environment *(Hogan, Pellegrini, and Microsoft 2021).*

W Sustainable meeting cultures are at the core of improving organizational ways of working. When collaborative behaviors are used effectively, time is both well spent and saved, which is fertile ground for transforming behaviors that enable effectiveness and operational excellence. While each company and workforce is distinct, this challenge affects all organizations that rely on their workforce to perform knowledge work.

Another finding to consider: The amount of time spent in meetings directly correlates to a company's headcount. When organizations exceed 1,000 employees, the average time an employee spends in meetings is approximately 12.8 hours per week. The average employee at companies with 200 to 999 employees and those with 10 to 199 employees spends about 10 hours per week in meetings *(Fellow 2024)*. Given that employees now spend an average of 11.3 hours a week in meetings, this adds up to approximately 392 hours per person per year. For companies, this means that meetings account for approximately 15 percent of total work time. A workforce feeling unproductive 15 percent of the time is costly for every organization. However, there are ways to create lasting benefits throughout your workflows, policies, and company culture. When we improve this specific aspect of our work habits, we create vast opportunities for how knowledge workers manage their time and how companies can better support them, resulting in significant benefits.

As we journey through the following phases of the WORK process, improving working methods will be our North Star, and changing our meeting culture and approach will be What we aim to do. The research above, combined with internal feedback on this specific work method and alignment with your company's purpose and approach, will provide the Why. In the next chapter, we will explore ways that teams can implement both large and small behavioral changes to transform the way work is done within teams and across broader organizations.

The exercises embedded within the WORK process help us identify workflows and behaviors that require transformation. Whether they need improvement, replacement, or complete reimagining, this process allows teams to experiment without feeling overwhelmed by significant change. Test theories, pilot new behaviors, and shift organizational mindsets without creating overwhelm and distraction long before deciding on new office designs, food programs, and events. Whatever is learned in the WORK phases informs what gets created in the succeeding PLACE phases. Remember: Behaviors come first. Places, spaces, and everything in between come later.

W *From Experience*

Walking Through Change and Toward Alignment

At the height of WeWork's rapid expansion, the company outgrew its New York headquarters in under a year. Originally designed for 1,200 people, it hosted over 1,800 employees daily, with new hires joining us each week. WeWork needed a workplace strategy, and fast.

My team was tasked with developing a new workplace strategy to reconfigure the physical environment to accommodate the growing number of employees working at and passing through headquarters each day—our What. This project was not just about designing a new HQ space; it was about creating more ease and access for WeWork employees to accomplish the company's goals and objectives while maintaining the pace required for work at a company in hypergrowth mode. We aimed to align with our greater company's Why: to help people create a life, not just a living.

Our HQ project team worked in stealth mode for over a month. We collected research, hosted interviews, and tested various scenarios to assess their viability before presenting our findings and formal recommendations to the C-suite. We explored four scenarios:

    1. Follow a traditional real estate strategy to relocate to a larger headquarters space.

2. Remove meeting rooms, lounges, and collaborative spaces to create more individual desk areas.

3. Permanently relocate back office teams to WeWork locations around the city to accommodate those teams that are growing fastest and are closest to the business's core.

4. Eliminate individual desks, opting for an unassigned Team Home model within a broader activity-based working environment.

If time had been on our side, we likely would have recommended Scenario 1. However, given our tight schedule, a twelve to eighteen-month process was just not feasible. The floor plans for Scenario 2 alone were...bleak. WeWork HQ was a vibrant and bustling place; putting rows and rows of desks would have instantly diminished that energy and risked part of what made WeWork so special at that time. Scenario 3, while common for large companies, would have created cultural consequences that far outweighed the project's technical success. Although Scenario 4 was the most complex option, it was the best choice for preserving the successful aspects of HQ while addressing some of the primary issues people frequently encountered. This option enabled us to create behavior-centric spaces, such as quiet zones for deep focus, extra lounge areas for collaboration, and brainstorming spaces with writable surfaces.

W In Scenario 4, we aimed to encourage the C-suite to adopt a new perspective on the workplace. For this to work, WeWork needed to think about the workplace as a comprehensive unit that all employees had access to, rather than just one small slice based on where their desk was located. In doing so, we would be able to create a shared ecosystem of spaces where people can be productive based on their tasks at hand, rather than having to make do with fewer options in a loud, open-plan environment. This approach also aligned perfectly with WeWork's mission at the time: Help people create a life, not just a living. We believed that enhancing ease and accessibility in the workplace would enable individuals to concentrate on what truly mattered to them, beyond merely fulfilling necessary tasks. At the time, WeWork was a leader in workplace innovation, Employee Experience, and the built environment. Since its inception, WeWork HQ has been a living lab, providing valuable insights for investors, potential clients, and partners, and Scenario 4 would continue that legacy.

We outlined the complexities of the challenge we faced and presented our proposal, carefully guiding the executive team through the various scenarios we had evaluated. We compared these scenarios against our priorities: acting quickly, minimizing disruption, and ensuring proximity. It was essential for the C-suite to understand the information in the same way we did and recognize that our proposed solution was the best option available given the constraints we faced. The C-suite agreed with us, and Scenario 4 began to take shape.

W

Our first action after receiving the green light was to build our coalition of supporters and partners. While our foundational strategy remained intact, we recognized the need for input from subject matter experts across the business to help us understand their teams' behaviors and needs, aligning them with project constraints. Because the change was complex and happening quickly, our success hinged on full support from leaders throughout the organization. The most effective way to revise our assumptions quickly was to share the same information we had provided to the C-suite.

In a conference room on one of HQ's main working floors, which we referred to as the HQ Change Studio, we printed large visuals for our C-suite presentation. We invited leaders from each team into the space, guided them through the project's rationale, and presented the proposed office layouts and designated spaces for their teams. After the presentation, they could provide feedback on whether their teams' working styles aligned with our workplace strategy. For teams that regularly handled confidential or highly sensitive information, we provided secure, off-site space at nearby WeWork locations as a supplement to their Team Homes located in HQ. This solution preserved the integrity of our all-access headquarters model while ensuring privacy for sensitive work without isolating teams or compromising the broader workplace strategy.

W

Given the project's constraints, everyone involved—including the core team—had to make concessions to succeed. While time was limited, proceeding with the original plan presented to the C-suite without adjustment would have risked delays, budget overruns, and the loss of support from both team leaders and executive sponsors. The HQ Change Studio played a crucial role in our change strategy. It helped us include team leaders in the project's early stages, offering them the opportunity to influence outcomes for their teams within the framework of the HQ change. Even during moments of frustration with our presentations, the leaders recognized that the project team was acting in good faith and working hard to meet the needs of various teams.

These Change Studio sessions laid the groundwork for how WeWork employees would engage with the next iteration of the living lab at HQ. Although space constraint was the catalyst for this change, we championed an employee-centered approach to the HQ transformation. We began to lay the groundwork for a deeper understanding of how high-collaboration and high-proximity teams can operate more dynamically with as little disruption to the day-to-day flow as possible.

– Corinne

8

Operationalize
Piloting Change To Learn Before Scale

TL;DR

Transformation succeeds when vision becomes structured pilot programs, not scaled initiatives. Pilots provide a controlled space for testing, gathering feedback, and iterating through two-way communication. With clear guardrails, defined ownership, and adaptive loops, people become co-creators of change, not passive recipients.

After defining the What and Why, and long before mass implementation, is piloting. Rather than launching broad, fixed initiatives, change starts in small, structured environments that allow for experimentation and learning. These dynamics enable feedback-driven refinement, help teams adapt concepts to real-world conditions, and prevent the disruption caused by sweeping changes. Early insights from pilots will help you validate the assumptions that shaped your experiments or reveal blind spots, shaping your next round of action.

This iterative process is essential for identifying and resolving potential challenges and enhancing strategies before concepts reach the entire workforce and the organization's complex structures. Sustained engagement with pilot teams is what turns planning into learning. Adapting concepts to the realities that teams face, based on feedback they provide, turns strategic concepts into clarified actions. This systematic approach provides a well-informed transformation that aligns with the organization's actual needs and dynamics, rather than assumptions and aspirations.

The Anatomy of a Pilot

At first glance, pilots may not seem strategic, but they often lead to better outcomes and significant cost savings than typical transformation initiatives. Pilot programs enable organizations to test assumptions, adjust, and build momentum that significantly increases change scalability and reduces failure rates *(McKinsey 2023)*. Once this methodology is adopted and actions compound, decisions are made faster, metrics clarify what's working, and insights guide What to scale. As you transition from one pilot to multiple ones, continued measurement becomes crucial.

Organizations often set ambitious behavioral goals but overlook piloting as a mechanism for enabling their gradual achievement. Time-boxed pilots create safe environments to test and refine ideas and protect critical operations from errors and unintended consequences during early phases. This approach enables teams to refine concepts with minimal disruption. Instead of broad changes requiring full buy-in, pilots facilitate shifts in smaller, manageable increments. Learning occurs in real time, and behavioral change becomes more sustainable through gradual adaptation.

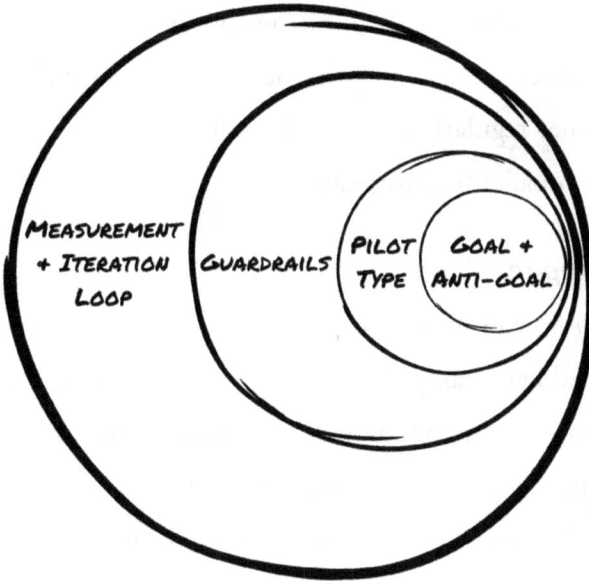

As part of pilot planning, it's critical to define clear goals and anti-goals. For example, if a pilot aims to increase productivity, an anti-goal might be to reduce the urge to multitask, and a goal might be to encourage workers to schedule deep focus hours. If employee satisfaction or effectiveness rises, that's worth tracking—but it's not the purpose. Defining these upper and lower boundaries helps everyone focus on what's important within the pilot. Participants give sharper feedback, communication becomes clearer, and the process runs more smoothly.

There are three key approaches to piloting that your transformation team can pursue:

Specialized Team Pilot

Piloting with teams that have unique workflows can be a powerful entry point because it allows for hands-on support. Tailoring efforts to their needs creates early buy-in and sparks a sense of change across the teams they regularly interact with, ultimately shaping the trajectory of the broader transformation.

Cross-Company Pilot

Unlike top-down organizational change, which implements a fully programmed new reality, cross-company piloting focuses on changing one behavior at a time across a workforce. This approach fosters momentum and enthusiasm from the outset of a transformation. For broad, foundational changes, it demonstrates that small shifts in how work is done can drive significant impact, without requiring large-scale disruption.

Team-Administered Pilot

Further along in a transformation cycle, when piloting structures are broadly understood, team-led piloting can help foster change across more teams simultaneously. Since this approach relies on manager or champion-led execution, upfront investment in training, feedback, and collaboration is crucial.

Depending on your transformation goals and available resources, these three pilot approaches can be utilized within a broader transformation effort. The challenge lies in maintaining consistency and continuity throughout the process.

Loose Frameworks

Experimental plans must diverge from traditional transformation models to thrive. More rigid approaches often fail under real-world conditions because they rely on static assumptions and linear processes. That's because they tend to presume consistency in variables that frequently shift as new insights emerge.

Loose frameworks offer an alternative approach that relaxes structures enough to infuse flexibility and adaptability without losing the core principles of change. They preserve the original vision without locking teams into a single path. As conditions shift, these frameworks adapt, offering guidance without prescribing every step, translating strategic intent into practical action, and supporting new behaviors through prototyping and testing.

Examples of loose frameworks include:

Relate

Share your What and Why with participants and invite them into the process of continuously improving initial ideas with their practical expertise. Address skepticism with empathy. Champions can help participants feel heard, especially when they understand how their feedback will shape the pilot and why it matters.

Simplify

To reduce information overload and change fatigue, distill pilot outcome intentions into a clear message with two to three actionable ways to accomplish it.

0

Facilitate

Support engagement with consistent touchpoints, milestone updates, and moments of reflection. Choose communication methods based on the desired outcome of each outreach, such as immersive events for engagement and surveys or interviews for feedback.

Prototype & Test

Piloting and prototyping are distinct but connected. Pilots create boundaries for testing, while prototypes offer the mindset to refine within them. Encourage participants to think in terms of iterations, rather than perfection. Some concepts that look strong during planning may not hold up in practice. Instead of starting over, identify what failed and why, and refine. Even small adjustments unlock major improvements.

Piloting requires a gardener mindset: You know your purpose and have some early ideas, but success depends on observation, validation, and iteration. You start with shared understanding—what works, what doesn't, and what you're trying to learn. Building a framework often reveals overlooked gaps. Let the group fill in those gaps together. Shared authorship fosters a stronger connection to the change. Loose frameworks accept life's twists and turns, and equip teams to learn and adapt as they grow.

Setting Guardrails & Identifying Owners

Although experimentation requires flexibility, boundaries and guardrails are essential to keeping each experiment focused, even as adjustments and adaptations occur. The goal is to stay directional without becoming rigid.

But not every aspect of a pilot is up for discussion or debate outside of a transformation team. Some constraints—such as financial limits, team bandwidth, and available resources—are nonnegotiable. Both pilot leaders and participants should thoroughly understand these core guardrails.

For example, time is the most critical constraint to maintain during the piloting process. When pilots have no clear endpoint or review process, they often calcify into untested norms. For smaller, well-contained efforts, a three-month minimum allows for two to three iteration cycles—enough to refine the concept meaningfully before considering broader rollout.

To preserve continuity, every pilot also needs a dedicated owner who guides the work, collects insights, and connects learning back to the overall transformation. Change Champions, who have been trained up and autonomized to lead in this capacity, can take on this new type of operational role. In addition, because of their pre-established role within their teams, Change Champions already have trust within their teams and can serve as strong local anchors for the process.

When defining pilot constraints, distinguish between what truly needs new structure and what can remain intact. For example, support ticket requests may increase due to a new strategy, but if the process already works to resolve them expediently, there's no need for redesign. In that case, simply reinforce the current policy when questions arise.

Reliable Communication for Experimental Exercises

Successful experimentation requires multidirectional communication, far beyond the usual top-down approaches, and with more frequency. Companies should use a range of communication methods to promote clarity and engagement across digital, physical, and experiential channels.

Information must consistently flow horizontally among participants and vertically from frontline teams to leadership to inform decisions and shape the direction of the work. Your communications should fulfill one of three key purposes:

Inform
Clarify the experiment's objectives (What) and rationale (Why) so participants understand its purpose and their role.

Engage

Encourage active participation by linking the experiment to behaviors that matter to the participants. Such engagement builds ownership and commitment.

Inquire

Gather feedback and perspectives to shape future iterations and improvements.

Strong feedback loops demonstrate that input is valued and enable continuous learning. Many change efforts fall short by under-preparing participants or overlooking their ability to shape outcomes. For pilots to succeed, participants need to know what's happening, how to engage, and how their input will influence the next steps.

Vary communication formats to cut through noise and sustain engagement. Utilize emails, town halls, chat tools, physical signage, workshops, and interviews tailored to the intended outcome—informing, engaging, or gathering information.

Purpose	Method	Location	Purpose Details
Inform	Email	Digital	High-level messaging and permanent reference point
Inform	Chat Message	Digital	Immediate, dynamic information sharing
Inform	Physical Signage	Physical	High-level messaging and permanent reference point
Inform	Town Halls	Physical & Digital	In-depth presentation of details for participants
Engage	Workshops	Experiential	Group brainstorming to integrate changes into workflows
Engage	Change Champion Networking	Experiential	Peer-to-peer information sharing
Engage	Intranet	Digital	Comprehensive, evergreen information repositories
Engage	Immersion Events	Physical	Simulations of the proposed end-state of changes
Inquire	Pulse Survey	Digital	Quantitative, of-the-moment feedback
Inquire	Retrospective Survey	Digital	Quantitative feedback from participants after significant milestone events
Inquire	Focus Groups	Experiential	Qualitative data from small cohorts within the experiment
Inquire	Interviews	Experiential	Qualitative data from individuals within the experiments

Tailor communication to your specific audience, considering how they absorb information best, and frame your message accordingly to ensure clarity, relevance, and impact.

- Executives need a concise summary of the pilot's purpose, scope, and alignment with company norms.

- Change Champions require the same summary, along with deeper context on rollout logistics, feedback collection, and responsibilities.

- Employees at all levels should hear how their earlier input shaped the initiative and what is being done with it.

- Pilot participants need all of the above, plus clarity on timing, roles, expectations, and guidance on messaging. Their engagement shapes broader perception, so transparency is key.

Pilot communication isn't a one-time push—it's cyclical. When feedback loops are active, participants become collaborators and co-creators of change, not just passive recipients. Shared authorship increases inclusion, commitment, and the likelihood of long-term success.

Piloting isn't a temporary phase—it's the foundation for lasting transformation. By structuring change as a series of experiments, organizations can reduce risk, build clarity, and generate trust before scaling new ways of working. Pilots translate abstract vision into real behavior, making it easier to adapt, iterate, and evolve. When change is tested in context and owned locally, transformation becomes not only possible but also sustainable.

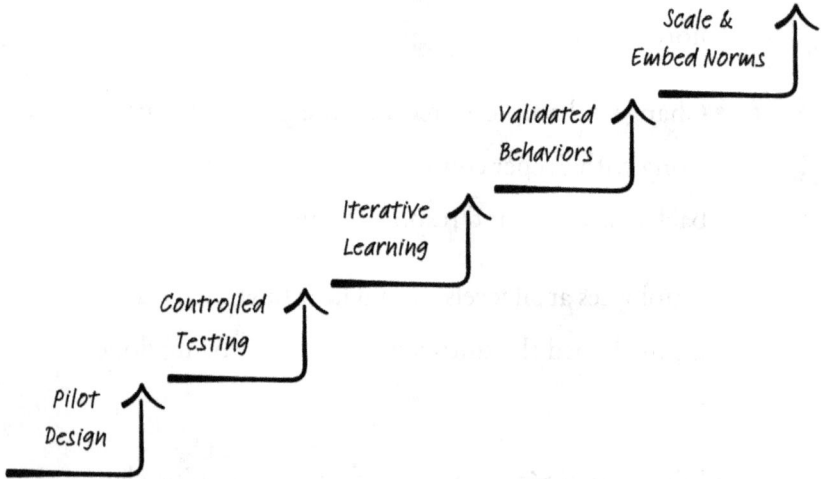

Pilot Design → Controlled Testing → Iterative Learning → Validated Behaviors → Scale & Embed Norms

In Theory

The Meeting Dilemma: Reducing the Reflex to Meet

0

Reducing meeting time requires more than a new policy. In recent years, companies like Dropbox and Shopify launched "meeting purges," while Asana piloted its now-famous "Meeting Doomsday." These initiatives weren't top-down mandates—they were the result of experiments.

In each case, small groups were asked to audit their calendars and evaluate which meetings added real value. Many recurring meetings didn't meet the new criteria for time, purpose, or participation and were temporarily removed. This reset functioned like a detox, giving employees the experience of a meeting-free calendar. Only after this pause could meetings be reintroduced—this time with clearer intent, reduced frequency, and updated expectations. The result was more time for focused work and more deliberate collaboration.

These audits eliminated low-value meetings, freeing up thousands of employee hours for more productive use. More importantly, they laid a foundation for rebuilding meeting culture from a clean slate that wasn't weighed down by outdated defaults. Asynchronous collaboration has become an increasingly popular alternative to real-time collaboration, especially in distributed teams. However, most interventions that promote it focus on eliminating meetings rather than transforming the behaviors that surround them. They address the symptoms—crowded calendars and disengagement—without changing the underlying habits that create them.

This isn't to say that all meetings are problematic. They keep teams aligned by providing the needed face-to-face interaction in hybrid and remote environments. Reducing or eliminating these in-person engagements can feel threatening because they offer the structure and connection that distributed work often lacks. Therefore, the goal is not to eliminate all meetings but to improve their quality and reduce their frequency. This approach supports greater autonomy, strengthens asynchronous work-flows, and fosters more intentional collaboration. But achieving this requires a behavioral change: clearer communication norms, consistent structures, and aligned priorities.

Pilot programs can help teams reshape meeting behaviors through structured, time-bound experiments. For example, a transformation team might lead a four-week "Meeting Reset Sprint" with clear rules:

- Pause all recurring meetings.
- Approve new meetings only when specific criteria are met.

- Default to asynchronous collaboration unless an escalation request has been validated due to urgency or complexity.

- Require each meeting to have a documented purpose, an attendee rationale, and a clear agenda; otherwise, participants can decline the invitation.

- Streamline meeting participation and outcomes with a universal agenda framework.

- Conduct weekly assessments to determine the value of existing meetings, support learning, and build shared norms.

These sprints enable teams to step back from habitual behaviors and re-enter with more intention and clarity, much like Asana's Doomsday approach. Unlike a static policy, this method functions as a live experiment, helping new habits take root without disrupting the entire organization.

To further support this shift, teams can introduce information request templates that help individuals clarify their needs before pulling others into meetings. This simple act of readiness fosters better habits over time, transforming collaboration into a conscious choice rather than a reflex.

From Experience

All the Time in the World

0

One of the most exciting change management projects I ever worked on began five years before the actual transformation was set to take place.

A New York City-based pharmaceutical company had quietly started selling its flagship headquarters near Grand Central Terminal and was selecting a new location in Hudson Yards. Before leadership could make a formal announcement, the *New York Post* broke the story, and word spread quickly among employees. What was intended as a confidential, long-lead real estate transaction suddenly became a crisis that required immediate attention. The new building hadn't even broken ground yet, but leaders needed to respond—quickly and thoughtfully—to a long-tenured workforce unaccustomed to sudden shifts.

My team was brought in to help craft a communications and change strategy that accomplished two key goals:

1. Address the upcoming move and how the news broke

2. Design a long-term engagement plan to help people interact meaningfully with the change without causing fatigue or frustration.

In most workplace transformations, communication efforts begin just a few months before a move and taper off shortly after. Yet, that window is often too narrow, resulting in one-way messages that announce decisions instead of building buy-in. For many employees, it's the first they're hearing about the change, and that delay breeds confusion or resistance.

However, in this case, time was on our side. We had five full years to design a transition plan that accounted for the many ways change would show up, especially for a workforce that valued stability. We broke the engagement strategy into five themed phases, each tailored to the stage employees were in during the change journey.

> **Year One** introduced the vision for the new head-quarters. To build early enthusiasm, we started with current leaders, rising stars, and nominated Change Champions.

> **Year Two** zoomed in from the neighborhood to the workplace itself, inviting employees to help shape the design strategy.

> **Year Three** involved testing new tools and work methods. Business units began piloting behaviors and technologies that would later define the new environment.

Year Four focused on the logistics of relocation. Employees received tactical guidance and support to prepare for the physical move.

Year Five marked the transition and evaluation phase, with new metrics and feedback channels in place to track how well employees adapted to their new space, tools, and practices.

To support this timeline, we built a diverse set of repeatable touchpoints across all five years. Our goal was to maintain a consistent flow of information without it becoming stale. We layered traditional tools—such as newsletters, surveys, and field guides, with experiential elements—including Hudson Yards tours and behind-the-scenes construction videos. We also introduced company-specific formats: executive Ask Me Anything (AMA) sessions and TED Talk–style briefings from project partners and design experts. This layered approach kept employees informed and engaged, while also providing them with opportunities to influence the outcome. It was the prototype version of the Inform, Engage, Inquire model outlined earlier in this chapter, applied over time and with increasing depth.

To make it work, we had to match our strategy to the natural rhythms of corporate life. We designed moments for high energy and visibility as well as quieter periods for reflection and reset. The result was a multidimensional engagement model that viewed change as a shared journey, rather than just an event. By pacing the process intentionally, we helped employees feel prepared not just for the move but for whatever came next. As a result, we strengthened their sense of partnership and trust in the organization's direction.

– Corinne

9

Regulate

Turning Pilot Wins Into Lasting Norms

TL;DR

Once behaviors are validated through pilot programs, they must be systematically incorporated into the organization. The Regulate phase codifies what worked and makes it stick. By clarifying key behaviors, mapping supportive resources, and aligning the broader system to make new patterns feel natural, outdated ones become difficult to maintain.

Pilots end—but change continues.

By the time pilots conclude, you'll have a clearer view of what worked and what's ready for broader adoption. The next step is turning those tested elements into lasting policies, norms, and expectations. Pilots must expand beyond isolated teams and begin to shape how the entire organization operates.

The Regulate phase evaluates what's ready to scale and facilitates motion. This phase is a translation process that uses insights gathered during piloting, including performance data and participant feedback, to identify which behaviors and systems are stable enough to become standard. As mentioned in the previous chapter, the loose frameworks approach, which accepts life's twists and turns, combined with multidirectional communication throughout the pilot, provides a well-rounded view of what's working and why.

R

This phase marks the moment when pilot concepts move from trial to reality. The transformation team must assess what improves quality, aligns with the strategic direction, and can withstand the test of time. Regulate isn't about preserving novelty—it's about embedding what works so change becomes durable.

Prepare for Change

Initiating the Regulation phase starts with a clear read on sentiment and performance. Evaluating pilot progress requires a blend of quantitative outcomes and qualitative insights, measuring alignment with strategic goals while capturing participants' lived experiences. Without this dual perspective, the pilot's full value and limitations remain obscured.

James Clear's *Atomic Habits* outlines five common behavior change barriers and provides strategies for overcoming them. While his framework is directed toward individuals in pursuit of personal improvement, effective organizational change can easily follow the same simple principles and resolve friction points that often become the main sources of resistance during scale.

Problem	Solution
Trying to change everything at once	Choose one thing, and do it well.
Starting with a change that's too big	Make the change so easy and appealing that you can't say no.
Seeking a result, not a ritual	Focus on the behavior, not the outcome.
Not changing your environment	Build an environment that promotes good habits.
Assuming small things don't add up	Get 1 percent better every day.

Regulation isn't just about formalizing success—it's about resolving what doesn't yet work. To guide this transition, apply the following principles:

Be Selective
Amplify and expand on what demonstrably worked, leaving the rest for a later date. Selectivity builds trust and avoids overwhelming the organization.

Simplify Complexities
Prioritize components that are intuitive and practical to adopt across teams.

Emphasize Behavioral Patterns

Surface the habits and mindset shifts behind success, not just outcomes or tools.

Identify Necessary Workplace Shifts

Document the physical, digital, and experiential changes needed to support new behaviors. These inputs feed directly into the phases in the *WORK then PLACE* process.

R

Celebrate the Incremental Wins

Acknowledge progress that's been made to build momentum and signal that change is taking hold.

Map where resistance is likely to surface. The data collected in earlier phases will help you spot friction points early. Develop targeted response strategies for potential issues that the transformation teams may encounter during this transitional phase. Sometimes, storytelling and transparency are enough to ease tensions or concerns. At other times, as seen in the What and Why phase, you may need to revise your recommendations based on feedback from key stakeholders. Pay close attention to which strategies shift resistance and why.

Before formalizing any pilot components, verify that your measurement mechanisms are capturing meaningful signals. Set baseline metrics for comparison and build simple dashboards that translate information into actionable insights for stakeholders, helping them understand the impact of piloting without getting lost in detail.

Regulation is a process of translation, not a switch to flip. Take time to confirm what's working, address what isn't, and clarify how you'll measure progress. Doing this well lays the foundation for successful scale and long-term adoption.

Address Resistance

R

Resistance to change is a natural response, especially among employees who are typically outside the sphere of influence when it comes to changes within a company. Studies show that employee resistance to change is attributed to the failure of more than 70 percent of large-scale transformations *(McKinsey 2023)*.

Remember, people naturally build habits and routines. When those are disrupted, resistance often follows. The Transtheoretical Model of Change reminds us that resistance isn't a detour; it's a predictable part of the transformation process. When resistance is anticipated and understood, it can become an opportunity to learn, align, and co-create, enabling a shift from current or outdated approaches to more effective ones.

Understanding Types of Resistance

Proactive resistance management begins with identifying its root causes. Employee resistance almost always stems from concerns about how change will affect their daily work and ability to be productive in their roles.

Systemic resistance arises when new initiatives clash with existing systems, workflows, or norms, creating procedural or structural friction. It's critical to distinguish these resistance types from influential resistance, as pushback from respected leaders or cultural carriers can shape broader organizational sentiment.

Engage with Resistance Directly

The first two principles of resistance management are simple: Never ignore them nor diminish them. Whether it arises from individuals or entire departments, address resistance directly with curiosity and respect. Facilitating open conversations will surface valid concerns that haven't been addressed elsewhere.

R

When people feel heard, they're more likely to engage, especially if you clearly explain how the transformation benefits both the business and its employees. Following up on these conversations proves that input leads to action and reinforces trust by insisting that change is a shared endeavor, not a top-down mandate.

When Resistance Requires Action

Not all resistance can—or should—be resolved through storytelling. Sometimes, concepts or workflows genuinely conflict with specific roles, locations, or operational realities. When flagged by employees or key stakeholders, this feedback deserves serious consideration.

Acknowledging valid resistance does two things: It helps the organization avoid costly missteps and reinforces trust in the transformation process. When people see their concerns taken seriously, they're more likely to stay engaged and contribute to meaningful solutions.

Transparency Through Data

Data is your strongest tool for addressing resistance. Let evidence, not assumptions, drive your adaptations. Transparent metrics ground the transformation rather than perception. Adopt a "show your work" approach by sharing data sources openly—as modeled by the WeWork HQ Change Studio—and bringing others into your reasoning and strategic vision.

This practice sustains the multidirectional communication established during pilots and limits speculation. The new challenge now is scale. How will these inputs guide decisions across the broader workforce? The Daisy model offers a practical lens for integrating data with real-world conditions.

Partner with Enablement Teams

When resistance stems from individual needs, rely on partners in your HR or People organizations to guide conversations. Their expertise in well-being, legal considerations, and equity complements your focus on operational design. Change Champions and direct managers can surface subtle issues early.

Throughout these exercises, safeguard the confidentiality of those who raise issues. Trust depends not just on what you communicate, but on how you protect people's experiences. Keep the focus on the transformation of workplace functionality and performance, rather than compliance or legal adjudication.

Evaluate Adaptation & Indicators

Effective evaluation begins not just with leadership intent, but with ongoing feedback from where the work is performed. Sentiments shift quickly. Without a grounded understanding of how work happens, measurement risks becoming guesswork.

Gather Data Systematically

To assess whether new ways of working are taking hold, you need insight into whether teams notice changes in their day-to-day effectiveness. In knowledge work that has not been distilled into tasks like sales, customer service, and software development, participant feedback will be your best data source.

Employee surveys designed to capture feedback in a quantitative, data-driven way can surface meaningful patterns that help you understand how people are experiencing what has been piloted.

Report Progress Effectively

Clear reporting is essential for aligning stakeholders and building trust through four key elements:

Intent
Clarify what's changing and why. Link the transformation to the company's North Star and offer context for anyone not involved in earlier pilots.

Objectives
Define what the changes aim to support, make this a consistent reference point for teams, and tie success to both business goals and employee needs.

Constraints & Guardrails

Name the limits—budget, timing, scope—to help manage expectations. Acknowledging boundaries builds credibility, especially when some outcomes won't be immediate.

Success Measures

Set clear metrics, but stay flexible. The right measures will align with your goals while leaving space for learning and course correction.

Most early data will be retrospective, but refined evaluation methods can begin to reveal forward-looking indicators over time. *WORK then PLACE* helps track long-term progress while scanning for emerging trends. With a thoughtful data strategy, evaluation becomes guidance for what comes next.

Adjust as Needed

Launching pilots into regulated norms marks the beginning of iteration and continuous improvement, not the completion of a single transformation. Pilots provide a foundation, but long-term success depends on refining ideas based on business-as-usual performance. For instance, consider how apps evolve—without regular updates, even groundbreaking tools can become obsolete. Continuous evaluation keeps solutions aligned with emerging needs.

Organizations that integrate continuous improvement practices into their operations see productivity and effectiveness gains of up to 25 percent compared to their peers *(McKinsey et al. 2024)*. Successful continuous improvement requires:

Maintain Flexibility Through Scaling

While universal approaches create consistency, effective change also requires contextual adaptation based on shifting knowledge work needs within your organization. Avoid excessive customization for specific cases. Exceptions introduce complexity, dilute measurement, and are hard to scale. If exceptions are required, then the core concepts that were piloted are not viable for broader organizational application.

When customization and exceptions do inevitably occur, clearly document them, identify recurring patterns, and pursue opportunities to strengthen your overall strategy. When handled thoughtfully, resistance becomes more than an obstacle—it becomes a strategic diagnostic.

Identify Necessary Changes

Moving from pilots to permanent policies requires more than surface-level tweaks. Adjusting, in this context, focuses on root-cause analysis and responding to feedback in ways that align with the broader transformation strategy. Rather than creating Band-Aid solutions for negative symptoms, prioritize foundational shifts that make new behaviors easier to adopt and sustain.

Oftentimes, data patterns reveal needs participants haven't

explicitly voiced. These unspoken insights can inform proactive solutions, helping you shape what's next before problems fully surface. With the right approach, transformation teams can operate strategically instead of reactively.

Keep in mind: People move between progress and setbacks. Thus, to maintain momentum, you must understand the expectations, habits, and friction points that drive behavior. Sustained engagement and timely feedback loops help you adjust the course before resistance hardens into a habit.

Implement Adjustments

Continuous improvement may sound straightforward, but building a culture that sustains it requires structure and care. Regular reviews, visible accountability, and capitalizing on easy wins help keep efforts focused on what employees truly need.

Then, when you implement adjustments, prioritize high-impact, low-friction changes that build confidence and momentum. In return, these small shifts often yield the biggest long-term gains and build endurance for complex, larger changes in the future.

But each adjustment deserves thorough testing before being rolled out. Skipping this step risks triggering unnecessary resistance—or undoing earlier progress. Keep validation cycles active and remain open to revision as new insights emerge.

Last, make sure to document what you learn. These reflections help teams distinguish minor execution issues from deeper design flaws. Define adjustments in behavioral terms—especially around collaboration, autonomy, and time—so change becomes measurable, repeatable, and scalable.

Activate for Impact

Unlike earlier phases, which focused on testing and refinement, this stage integrates successful pilot outcomes into the organization's everyday operations.

R

Solidify the New Foundation

Metrics and measurements must evolve into the embedded new behaviors of your company's culture. Experimental indicators established in pilots must eventually transition into stable metrics that shift the focus to accountability and long-term governance. Then ownership must transition from the transformation team to permanent business partners to maintain continuity and anchor new behaviors and mindsets in daily operations.

Keep in mind: A transformation becomes real when pilot teams, leaders, and sponsors can demonstrate visible, measurable progress toward the original goals.

Expand Reach and Impact

With the foundation set, it's time to scale. At this juncture, you can choose to launch this part of the effort among select teams, gradually implementing new behaviors, or launch across the whole company simultaneously, depending on your transformation goals, timelines, and available resources. Along the way, implement the feedback loops established earlier in the pilot to resolve friction points as they arise.

Expansion adds a new dynamic as pilot participants become teachers. Having co-created and lived through the early stages of change, Change Champions now act as guides for their peers and advocates for groups just being introduced to the pilots and new behaviors. Change Champions don't parrot talking points; they share stories, data, missteps, pivotal moments, and the tangible wins. Their firsthand insight adds nuance and credibility to the operational leadership of Project Owners, building trust among employees that is necessary for scaling change throughout the organization.

Transition to Permanence

Successful practices now need to be anchored inside the business, where they are managed and refined over time.

For this to happen, Change Champions step into expanded roles as Pilot Owners, to guide adoption and build new skills in change leadership, communication, and behavioral design. The transformation team supports them with training and tools, particularly in areas such as reporting and adapting to variations. Keep in mind: Change Champions don't replace core operators in this new ownership model. Instead, they help support them through the change. Pilot Owners work within existing team structures and functions, embedding transformation into daily routines. As each new cohort expands, it builds momentum and shifts the broader organizational mindset.

Eventually, responsibility shifts from time-bound Pilot Owners to long-term Norm Owners—individuals or teams embedded in functions such as Business Operations, HR, or Workplace. Like product managers, they steward the practices established during transformation. This transition requires formal knowledge transfer—not just guides and playbooks, but durable infrastructure, such as repositories, records, and living documentation—that sustain progress despite turnover or strategic shifts.

R

The Regulate phase is the bridge between experimentation and lasting transformation. As teams move through this part of the *WORK then PLACE* process, they shift from testing ideas to embedding them, turning promising pilots into norms that endure well beyond the initial wave of enthusiasm.

Of note: This stage demands both rigor and empathy. Data must guide decisions, but lasting adoption hinges on how resistance is handled and how progress is communicated. Success isn't about rollout speed—it's about whether the changes feel intuitive, relevant to employees, and sustainable.

The shift from Pilot Owners to Norm Owners reflects a deeper transition from temporary initiative to institutional capability. By the end of this phase, transformation teams will have ushered in new processes and a more resilient, responsive organization. You'll know the change has taken root when new practices feel natural and the old ones are barely remembered. That's when transformation becomes identity—woven into how the organization thinks, works, and grows.

As you prepare to move from the WORK phases into PLACE, keep this in mind: The behavioral systems you solidify now will shape everything that follows. Get this phase right, and the next ones don't just work—they build on a foundation strong enough to carry lasting change.

R

In Theory

The Meeting Dilemma: Testing Your Way to Better Meeting Culture

Transforming meeting culture hinges on experimenting with what actually works for your organization's unique needs. Issuing mandates does not change behaviors, but piloting new concepts does. Organizations that have made real progress didn't begin with ideal solutions. Instead, they started by asking questions like: "What happens if we remove all recurring meetings?" "How can employees reclaim unscheduled time?" and "What would it take to justify the cost of a meeting?"

These companies treated meetings not as a fixed structure but as a system—something they could observe, modify, and evolve. Below are three post-pandemic experiments that any organization can adapt, remix, or test.

Meeting Cost Calculators: Assigning Value to Time

In 2023, Shopify implemented a cost-estimating tool directly into employees' calendars to create more visibility around the cost of labor within each meeting *(Bloomberg News, Gindis, and Boyle 2023)*. This experiment made abstract costs concrete and encouraged intentionality before scheduling. For example, a short meeting with a few mid-level employees might cost over $1,000; including an executive could double that figure. By highlighting the

R

monetary weight of time, Shopify created a friction point that made unnecessary meetings harder to justify.

What you can try:

- *Build a simple calculator using average salary data and integrate it into calendar requests.*
- *Encourage team leads to review meeting costs in their retrospectives or planning cycles to create more awareness.*

No-Meeting Days: Creating Rhythms for Focus

Slack's "Focus Fridays" and Shopify's meeting-free Wednesdays allowed employees to have full days dedicated to deep work *(Slack and Elliot 2022)*. The goal was not to eliminate meetings forever but to rebalance the rhythm of the workweek. Slack also introduced "Maker Weeks," which allow for entire periods of creativity, development, and focused work. These weeks function like mini-sabbaticals, giving employees cognitive space without requiring a complete pause from work.

What you can try:

- *Establish a no-meeting day within each department or team.*
- *Run quarterly "Focus Weeks" for experimentation and innovation.*
- *Track productivity and stress levels before, during, and after these initiatives.*

Meeting Eligibility Criteria: Redefining What Deserves Synchronous Time

Dropbox established clear criteria for when to hold a meeting: When a decision, debate, or discussion needed to be had. This clarity simplifies the social ambiguity around whether a meeting is necessary and empowers employees to opt out if the agenda doesn't meet those criteria *(Dropbox, n.d.)* It also enables boundary-setting and accountability without relying on hierarchical structures. For example, instead of saying, "I'm too busy," employees can respond, "This topic is better resolved asynchronously."

R

Virtual First: Effectiveness Kit

Meetings 101

Do you really need that meeting?

✓ Keep meetings for the 3d's

3d's = important decisions, debates, and discussion

One-way door decisions.
Irreversible choices, like who to hire as your next COO.

Big debates.
Should your primary brand color be blue or green?

Getting unblocked.
You've been going back and forth, but you can't make progress.

Creative brainstorming.
Generating ideas for your next campaign.

Kick-offs, first-time meetings, and 1:1s.
When you need to build trust, face time can help.

Sensitive or challenging topics.
Personal issues or performance feedback.

⊗ Handle non-3d meetings async

Say it over chat, email, or a doc.

Status updates and FYIs.
Send info shares with your project management tool, email, or chat.

Getting feedback or support.
Ask them to review it in a doc, or send a support request via Jira/Epic.

Sharing a proposal.
Write a (concise) draft in a doc, then gather feedback asynchronously.

Two-way door decisions.
Should the button say "buy" or "purchase"?

Quick, straightforward questions.
Such as: When does your team want to have the next meeting?

(Dropbox, n.d.)

What you can try:

• *Publish a straightforward meeting scheduling rubric.*

• *Add mandatory "purpose labels" in calendar invitations: Is this for a decision, debate, or discussion?*

Experiments are valuable not only for the changes they bring about but also for revealing friction points, habits, and misunderstandings that impede effective collaboration. By treating meetings as prototypes rather than defaults, organizations can reduce waste while increasing quality.

R

From Experience

Snack Mastery

One of Hulu's top business objectives in its early days was to foster creativity and innovation. As a company, we had a clear purpose: to innovate the streaming world, and the workplace concepts that encourage creativity in all areas of the company.

R

Fast forward to 2018, when the food and beverage budget per person was $5 per day, and the Workplace Experience team wanted to invest in ways that would pay dividends to the company's North Star and commitment to creativity and innovation. For some context, the food and beverage budgets at most major technology companies total over $ 20 per person daily, but that's because these companies often lack opportunities to craft unique gatherings with teammates around something other than work. Although Workplace Experience teams are rightly focused on removing frictions from employees' days, the cost of becoming so efficient also eliminates the character that maintain company culture and memorable employee experiences.

Nevertheless, instead of providing the tech industry's standard of free, made-to-order meals, Hulu decided to zig where others tended to zag. Local restaurants were invited onto campus to serve meals at a subsidized cost, making it extremely affordable for Hulu employees to sample a variety of cuisines from the diverse culinary world of Los Angeles. And because they chose to subsidize meals instead of making them free, Hulu's Workplace Experience team was able to offer a wide array of free snacks, ranging from the more traditional snack packs of pretzels and granola bars to the more substantial options like fruit, hummus, hard-boiled eggs, cheeses, cured meats, breads, and much more.

Almost immediately, Hulu employees began crafting full meals out of the snack supply. Everything from grilled cheese sandwiches, caprese salads, breakfast burritos, nachos, and even casseroles. Teams also began holding gatherings in the company's pantry, where the challenge was to create the best hors d'oeuvres using only the pantry's ingredients. Eventually, a team gathered the recipes and created the Hulu cookbook, an amalgamation of the best, the weirdest, and just plain disgusting dishes concocted by Hulu employees. While there was occasional wishing for free meals, the snack pantry put people's minds at ease for a short time each day, drew people together, and—although it can't be proven—likely drove creativity.

Most companies prioritize providing their people with well-fueled meals quickly so they can return to their work replenished and ready, prioritizing easy access to sustenance over communal time with colleagues. As renowned game designer Mark Rosewater said, "Restrictions breed creativity." When you restrict something, especially a fundamental element of human needs, such as food, creativity is almost guaranteed. Although office snacks are not directly correlated with employee productivity or company profits, the creativity and willingness to experiment were a clear demonstration of how Hulu put their goals into action, even in the smallest ways.

- Sara

R

10

Knowledge Base

Documenting What Works For Everyday Guidance

TL;DR

Pilots yield insights, but only documentation turns them into long-term value. The Knowledge phase converts lessons into systems, tools, and shared reference points. When done well, this work makes change sustainable by embedding learning into daily operations.

For the transition from pilots to permanence to succeed, behavioral insights must be institutionalized as intelligence and preserved in practical, usable Knowledge Bases that are accessible to the workforce. Strong Knowledge Bases support real work; they are easy to access, built around common tasks, and structured in ways that people can learn—through systems, search, and storytelling.

This phase organizes learnings into durable resources across three practices:

- Designing Systems & Infrastructure

- Organizing for Accessibility

- Maintenance & Evolution

These areas help pilot-tested ways of working thrive beyond the transformation effort. That's because developing and maintaining Knowledge Bases allows teams to navigate change confidently, informed by reliable, current, and intuitive materials. These resources serve as the foundation for ongoing transformation.

Within an organization's information ecosystem, Knowledge Bases fill the gaps between generalized employee handbooks and tactical standard operating procedures. They consist of employee training, internal systems maps, cultural records, and other related materials. Overall, Knowledge Bases capture the components of an organization's success, its effects, and the case for changes and adjustments.

Designing Systems & Infrastructure

A strong Knowledge Base begins with well-designed information systems. These are more than technologies or tools—they're a network of processes, platforms, templates, and documented behaviors that embed new ways of working into daily operations. Building this infrastructure requires your attention on three interconnected elements:

Identify Required Tools

Start by cataloging existing resources—documents, communications, pilot takeaways, team feedback—and note what's missing. From there, outline the essential artifacts required to provide operational clarity, including decision logs, workflow diagrams, policy clarifications, and training modules. Every artifact should include a TL;DR or other concise summary of what it is and its purpose for easy reference.

Remember: Uncovering gaps is part of this process, not a setback. Every point of confusion now could become a barrier for someone later. Use these signals to instead refine and stabilize your materials. For example, before designing sophisticated solutions, explore low-fidelity, quick-to-deploy tools that validate your processes and behaviors. Save heavier tech investments for later, and only after simpler solutions have been proven insufficient.

Establish Supporting Processes

Tools that enable Knowledge Bases only work when connected to clear processes about how work is done within your company. Well-defined and integrated systems create clarity by outlining how tools are used, by whom, and under what conditions. Start with how Knowledge Bases will guide people on:

- **Onboarding Protocols:** to introduce new employees to behavioral and cultural norms.

- **Exception Handling:** to address deviations without eroding consistency.

- **Feedback Loops:** to capture issues, suggestions, and points of friction.

Validate each approach with people unfamiliar with the work to determine viability and utility. If a newcomer can't follow it, neither will your future workforce.

Store materials in a centralized, searchable location, such as a wiki or internal knowledge hub that is consistently monitored and maintained to guarantee information integrity. Instead of PDFs or other static files, guide people to live document links that are automatically refreshed without the need for removal or updates.

Implement Technology Integration

Once the preliminary Knowledge Base infrastructure is in place, revisit your system design to assess where technology can help make resources more accessible to employees. Prioritize platforms that:

- Reinforce proven workflows.

- Automate or streamline routine steps without adding friction.

- Provide insight into system usage and adherence.

Don't waste time searching for perfect systems, just choose what works and will offer a clear benefit to your teams.

Organizing for Accessibility

Because Knowledge Bases are data repositories and tools for comprehension, adoption, and empowerment, accessibility and ease of use are paramount to their success. If information is difficult to find, confusing to read, or lacks context, it fails its core purpose. Accessibility, both in terms of structure and language, transforms a static archive into a dynamic resource.

Apply Universal Design Principles

Documentation should support a range of roles, workflows, and learning needs. For example, IKEA furniture manuals use visuals, anticipate confusion, and work globally with minimal text, making their products as universally accessible as possible. When developing Knowledge Bases, follow these core design principles:

- **No Gatekeeping:** Avoid permission-based access or insider-only systems.

- **Logical Placement:** Group content by natural associations and adjacent tasks.

- **Plain Language:** Cut jargon. Aim for clarity, not cleverness.

- **Multi-format Support:** Pair written guidance with diagrams, videos, or checklists for enhanced learning and comprehension.

Always write with first-time users in mind. What context do they need? Where do people typically get lost? Address those points directly.

Use the LATCH Framework

Good organization reduces cognitive load, which is essential for people's capacity to internalize what they learn and how to apply it in their day-to-day work. In his book *Information Anxiety*, Richard Saul Wurman, who coined the term "information architecture," outlines his LATCH framework and the five intuitive structures that create a common organizing language:

K

- **Location:** For geographically distinct content or site-based practices.

- **Alphabetical:** Ideal for glossaries or contact lists.

- **Time:** Use for rollout schedules or historical tracking.

- **Category:** Best for templates, toolkits, or policies by function.

- **Hierarchy:** Prioritize by importance or sequence; e.g., "Start Here". *(Wurman 1989)*

Most systems benefit from combining methods. For example, process guides might use hierarchy and category, while directories use alphabetical or location-based formats. Consistency matters more than structure—choose approaches that are intuitive and repeatable.

Offer Multiple Access Points

Different users need different levels of detail. Create layered entry points for each section:

- TL;DR summaries for quick reference.

- Checklists for task execution or compliance.

- Full-length documents for comprehensive understanding.

For instance, a new hire might want the full download of information when they join the company, while a tenured employee may just need one step confirmed. Build for both extremes. Co-design your Knowledge Bases with Change Champions and early adopters, as they know where confusion hides and how people use the information in real time. Consider piloting the Knowledge Base itself to test its viability, just as you did with the piloted behaviors that preceded it.

Maintenance & Evolution

Once the Knowledge Base is live, the work shifts from creation to stewardship. These resources must evolve in step with the organization, and need to be updated, augmented, expanded, and clarified as behaviors and conditions shift. While the transformation team establishes the foundation, sustained impact depends on structured handoffs and committed ownership to keep the Knowledge Base active, relevant, and trusted.

Implement Governance Structures

To preserve the momentum of change, governance should be intentional but not burdensome. Ownership of the Knowledge Base should shift from the transformation team to long-term enablement functions, such as HR, People Operations, IT, or Real Estate. Just as pilots become norms, Knowledge Bases must transition into embedded systems managed through distributed stewardship:

- Assign **Stewards** to manage specific content areas and ensure their relevance.

- Define **Escalation Paths** for resolving disputes or ambiguities.

- Set **Review Cadences** that align with the pace of business change.

Governance roles integrate into existing workflows to establish continuity without bureaucracy.

Conduct Cyclical Reviews

Knowledge Bases lose value when left static. Schedule regular evaluations—quarterly, semiannually, or annually—based on the rate of evolution in each content area and trigger additional reviews in response to major organizational changes such as restructures, new tools, or policy shifts.

K

Each review should assess:

- **Accuracy:** Are the tools, policies, and processes still current?

- **Accessibility:** Is the information easy to find and use?

- **Clarity:** Have new questions or misunderstandings emerged?

The functional owner of each content area should document updates and communicate key changes to relevant audiences.

Manage Documentation Evolution

As your organization matures, some content will need simplification while other elements will require retirement. Develop clear systems for documenting lifecycle management:

- **Archive** outdated walkthroughs and retain concise summaries.

- **Condense** long guides into streamlined onboarding resources.

- **Link** deprecated content to historical repositories for continuity of context.

Calibrate your documentation depth based on team needs. For example, high-growth or high-turnover teams may benefit from more detail, while mature teams often prefer brevity.

Leverage Change Champion Networks

Change Champions provide crucial continuity because they hold institutional memory about why norms were established, where friction persists, and how behaviors have evolved. Engage Change Champions in review cycles to:

- Track adoption and relevance.

- Surface user pain points and usage gaps.

- Support transitions, onboarding, and content updates.

Change Champions serve as internal amplifiers, helping to ensure the Knowledge Base reflects real work as it happens.

K

Above all: Work must precede Place. This principle anchors sustainable transformation for modern companies navigating the uncertainty of business in the 2020s. Despite the common practice of enacting change, the physical environment, especially in hybrid or Return to Office scenarios, often yields lasting change from behavioral norms, rather than floor plans. The Knowledge Base makes those behavioral shifts concrete. Once new ways of working are codified, physical environments can be oriented to support them—intentionally, not reactively.

By prioritizing behavior-first rationale, companies avoid costly design missteps and build spaces that reflect actual needs. Revisit your "Define Your Why" work as needed—if operational guidance doesn't resolve a question, the Why should serve as your compass.

You'll know the Knowledge Base is working when it disappears into the background; when employees stop asking where to find information, when onboarding feels seamless, and when change feels intuitive rather than enforced.

Knowledge Bases are not intended to document everything. Instead, they embed information that promotes behaviors that enable effectiveness and success within your organization. Accomplishing this takes discernment, context, and a deep understanding of what teams need to succeed. That's the true aim of the WORK phase: Building lasting organizational capability to sustain and evolve transformation, even after the pilot team has stepped away.

K

In Theory

The Meeting Dilemma: Documentation That Sustains & Amplifies Change

Behavior change that is not embedded in an organization's operational memory is unsustainable. Even the strongest initiatives fade without shared language, repeatable processes, and institutional memory. In this phase of transformation, documentation isn't overhead—it's infrastructure.

K

Companies like Dropbox, Asana, and Slack didn't just pilot new ways of working; they recorded what worked and how to sustain it. Internal guides clarified roles, timing, and decision points, served as roadmaps for adoption, and made it more difficult to revert to default behaviors.

Internal Documentation: A Shared Compass

Dropbox's *Virtual First Toolkit* gives employees reference points for every phase of collaboration, including communication norms, decision-making protocols, and documentation standards. Asana's *Meeting Doomsday* playbook includes a meeting necessity checklist and scripts for professionally declining unnecessary invites.

What you can do:

- *Build a "Meeting Manual" tailored to your culture— include norms, cancellation criteria, and stories from your pilots.*

- *Create a shared digital space (e.g., internal wiki or Notion) for meeting best practices and update it regularly with team input.*

Public Sharing: Strengthening the Field

When companies publish their methods and findings, they contribute to a broader shift in how work is conducted. This transparency builds reputational trust, encourages peer learning, and signals to employees that they're part of something bigger. As the body of shared knowledge expands, so does its impact, allowing for evolution beyond organizational change to cultural change.

What you can do:

- Publish lessons from successful pilots through blog posts, webinars, or conferences.

- Invite other organizations to test your methods and offer feedback.

Meeting culture is notoriously difficult to change—and even harder to maintain. However, with thoughtful documentation, companies can connect behavior, belief, and policy, ensuring that progress becomes the new norm, not a temporary phase.

From Experience

To Know or Not to Know: The Cost of Unusable Information

As part of onboarding new vendors, a client in the technology industry required consultants and service providers to read more than seventy documents outlining scopes, processes, and contextual materials. The intention was understandable—previous vendors had consistently misunderstood or misapplied requirements, resulting in costly misalignments and high churn rates. Leadership believed that flooding partners with information would prevent future errors. However, volume doesn't equate to clarity, and documentation—without structure, hierarchy, or relevance—doesn't lead to understanding.

To achieve alignment from the start, the client believed comprehensive reading would prevent future confusion. They believed that a lack of information was the root of the problem, and their solution was to provide more of it. However, sheer volume does not equal clarity, and documentation does not inherently result in understanding, especially if it isn't structured for effective day-to-day use.

The archive included statements of work, preventive maintenance protocols, escalation procedures, and compliance norms. It was exhaustive, but not cohesive. Even diligent vendors were

K

175

unsure what to prioritize, what was current, or how the pieces fit together. As a result, instead of reducing ambiguity, the documentation deepened it. There was no clear map for success.

Our team chose to approach this differently. Rather than slogging through disconnected files, we reorganized the content into something usable: a distilled, three-page playbook. It included:

- A summary of expectations

- What success looks like

- How we can make you look good

Each requirement was mapped to the appropriate internal teams, transforming vendor work from interpretive guesswork to strategic alignment. As a result, everyone used the same reference. Confusion dropped. Speed increased. Trust grew.

This clarity eliminated friction and created space for creativity. Teams could ask, "What's the best way to meet this need here and now with these people?" That question led to smarter experimentation, better outcomes, and faster learning.

One example: During HVAC maintenance planning, we applied the TL;DR approach to document expectations and success metrics.

Short Summary of Expectation (TL;DR)	What Success Looks Like *How do we make you look good?*
Preventive Maintenance— HVAC	• Increased ease of completion of regular maintenance exercises. • Five-year forecast of end-of-life mechanical replacement requirements.

Teams were able to experiment with new scheduling strategies, trial a smarter tagging system, and even pilot predictive maintenance without scope creep. They moved from merely interpreting a policy to delivering results. We used this same model for the team's workspace operations scope, helping the client define and achieve their key performance indicators.

K

Short Summary of Expectation (TL;DR)	What Success Looks Like *How do we make you look good?*
Key Performance Indicators (KPIs) are achieved 85% of the time. KPIs are:	What needs to be seen 85% of the time:
Workspaces Effectiveness	Ensure preventive and reactive maintenance tickets are completed on time with minimal unplanned downtime (limited to 15%, which was later revised to 1% based on clarity in the goal).
Fiscal Responsibly	Deliver budgets within 3% of projections.
Continuous Improvement	Save at least 1% of the annual fee each quarter.

177

Originally, 15 percent downtime was acceptable. However, that benchmark didn't reflect the reality of this high-performance environment. Once clarified, the target dropped to one percent. This precision enabled the client and our team to focus attention and create alignment, leading to unexpected and powerful wins.

During a routine site walk, the vendor observed that nearly one-third of private rooms were consistently booked for use but rarely occupied. Together, we chose to make these rooms available for general use, with no booking system required. Within a year, the benefits of this change were:

- A six-figure cost benefit thanks to better space utilization
- Increased space availability for those who needed it
- Avoided the cost of hiring a firm for an expensive utilization study

The team achieved its savings target by prioritizing clarity and brevity, and by creating a system of shared understanding that linked expectations to roles, outcomes, and actions that helped the client reframe static information into living tools. This transformation reduced vendor churn and created a shared foundation for decision-making and trust.

The key takeaway: Information isn't power unless it's usable.

- Sara

SECTION THREE:

P.L.A.C.E.

The behaviors piloted and normalized in WORK are then brought to life through PLACE. Once behavioral norms are established, the physical, digital, and experiential environments are designed to reinforce what is aligned with your company's North Star. While PLACE isn't where transformation begins, it is where it becomes visible, repeatable, and measurable.

With behaviors tested and adopted, PLACE translates intention into infrastructure. It includes office layouts, collaboration platforms, communication systems, and workflow tools anywhere work happens. When done well, PLACE multiplies success throughout your organization. Done prematurely, it only adds noise and disconnection within your workforce.

PLACE becomes effective through five structured steps:

1. **Position** environments in alignment with behavioral norms.

2. **Leverage** existing tools and assets before adding complexity.

3. **Adapt** space and systems to fit the work, not the other way around.

4. **Catalyze** assets by calculating needs, categorizing use, and configuring accordingly.

5. **Evolve** through continuous use, feedback, and iteration.

Like the chapters that precede it, PLACE concludes with a case study, demonstrating how behavioral clarity leads to environmental strategies that are not only functional but also enduring. When rooted in supporting real organizational behaviors—not just aspirations—PLACE enables the work employees do, rather than just being the container for it.

11

Position

Mapping The Workplace Ecosystem To Behavior

TL;DR

Positioning maps behavioral needs to the physical, digital, and cultural environments of work. It highlights what supports people, what hinders them, and how they are underutilized. Aligning your environment with how people actually work creates the foundation for intentional, sustainable change.

Position uncovers the often invisible systems that shape behavior and builds a grounded roadmap for aligning the environment with organizational intent. Too frequently, space planning and systems upgrades are treated as isolated decisions. When disconnected from behavioral reality, they introduce friction instead of flow. This phase shifts the approach; begin with what's real, not what's aspirational. What's working? What's outdated, misaligned, or missing?

Diagnostic mapping helps you assess your workplace through the lens of daily behavior, not general preference.

Position is not a prompt to redesign. Instead, it's a call for clarity on what enables performance, what gets in the way, and what could be leveraged differently. You'll evaluate your workplace through three lenses: amplifiers, inhibitors, and neutrals—each revealing distinct paths for action.

Many workplace strategies begin with assumptions; executives identify pain points, implement fixes, and hope that behaviors will adjust over time. Position reverses that pattern. Instead of starting with what's broken, begin with what's working. Use pilot learnings and documented insights to evaluate your current environment while grounding the rest of the PLACE process—Leverage, Adapt, Catalyze, and Evolve—in behavioral evidence.

P

The Cross-Functional Workplace

Workplaces span multiple functions: Real Estate manages space, IT owns the digital stack, and HR and Communications shape culture and experience. However, employees don't engage with these systems in isolation—they experience them as part of a single, interconnected environment.

Effectively aligning your workplace with the behaviors that support organizational success is a cross-functional exercise. Position makes the alignment intentional and visible by using the behavioral data collected during the WORK phases to map against current environments, highlighting disconnects, reinforcements, and missed opportunities.

IT may implement a platform that streamlines digital collaboration, but if Real Estate maintains open-concept spaces that amplify noise, these systems and the behaviors they support clash. This contradiction undermines effectiveness because, although both systems might perform well in isolation, their unintegrated combination creates misalignment and frustration within the workforce. Position reveals these incongruencies early, enabling strategic adjustments in later phases.

P

Begin by mapping your resources across the physical, digital, and experiential domains in relation to the four types of knowledge work introduced in Chapter 3. This map will reveal where your suite of offerings aligns with or contradicts your documented behaviors, and whether they support or contradict one another.

	Physical	Digital	Experiential
Synchronous Collaboration	Team Spaces Meeting Rooms Phone Booths Breakout Spaces AV Systems	Productivity Suites (Office 365, Google Workspace) Conferencing Tools Workspace Booking Tools	Hybrid Work policies Meeting Culture policies Smart Scheduling policies
Asynchronous Collaboration	Individual Desks Quiet Spaces	Productivity Suites Communication Tools	Workflow Management policies Collaboration frameworks
Individual Focus	Individual Desks Quiet Spaces	Productivity Suites	Do Not Disturb policies Time Management norms
Socializing	Cafés Break Rooms Lounges	Booking tools for social spaces	Company rituals Team Gathering guidelines

P

The Physical Ecosystem

When evaluating your physical environment, begin by identifying the type(s) of knowledge work each space was intended to support, and whether those intentions align with the behavioral norms established in the WORK phases. Misalignment will be addressed later; this stage is about creating clarity.

Identify spaces that act as behavioral amplifiers, those that visibly support. Then enable the documented norms you're scaling, such as flag inhibitors, spaces that undermine or confuse the norms, and neutrals that neither help nor harm. When employees clearly understand how a space supports their work, it becomes a functional part of the workplace behavior system, not just a backdrop.

The Digital Ecosystem

Technology shapes work patterns just as powerfully as the built environment. Each tool you deploy comes with embedded assumptions about how people communicate, make decisions, and track progress. These assumptions may reinforce or contradict the behavioral norms you've already validated.

Evaluate whether your tools support the behaviors that your pilots have proven successful. If asynchronous decisions have improved team focus, do your platforms facilitate them, or do they default to live meetings? If transparency sped up delivery, are your tools set up to make sharing information seamless?

As with physical space, identify digital amplifiers, or tools that reinforce desired behaviors, as well as inhibitors, or tools that force workarounds and encourage regressions to outdated habits. Most digital ecosystems evolve without a system-wide strategic plan as they layer tool upon tool until friction and inertia become the norm. Position gives you the clarity to articulate this pattern to inform future changes.

The Experiential Ecosystem

Your workplace culture—expressed through policies, norms, and expectations—shapes behavior more pervasively than space or tools. These cultural systems determine how decisions are made, how information is disseminated, and what behaviors are rewarded or discouraged.

Evaluate whether your current experiential systems support the behaviors you've identified as drivers of success. If your culture values speed and distributed authority, do your approval processes reflect that? If transparency improves outcomes, are your communication expectations aligned?

Look for the amplifiers in your culture—rituals, handbooks, or reward systems that reinforce good behavior. Now name the inhibitors—unclear expectations, unspoken norms, outdated policies, or misaligned incentives that create friction and confusion.

P This diagnostic process identifies the workplace elements that are already amplifying effective behaviors and where untapped opportunities exist to enhance your workplace strategy. Most importantly, it fosters a shared understanding of the workplace across Real Estate, HR, and IT, shifting the conversation from functional ownership to shared responsibility and continuous impact.

By evaluating the workplace through the lens of behavior, your organization moves beyond implementing isolated upgrades to a unified, evidence-based strategy. This cross-functional clarity sets the foundation for the remaining PLACE phases, where enhancements, adaptations, and innovations will be built on organizational reality rather than assumptions.

Governance for Ongoing Evaluation

Positioning evolves from a one-time event into a sustained organizational capability when governed by clear ownership structures, decision-making protocols, and review processes. Effective governance ensures that your workplace remains aligned with the behaviors critical to organizational success as conditions continue to evolve, long after the *WORK then PLACE* process concludes.

Cross-functional governance enables Real Estate, HR, and IT to transition from parallel, uncoordinated execution to an orchestrated impact. It allows these functions to assess how their decisions influence the integrated system, rather than measuring the progress of their domain in isolation. Shared accountability must shift from utilization and compliance metrics to indicators that link workplace inputs—spaces, tools, policies—with observed behavioral outcomes established during the WORK phases.

Because behaviors and the systems that support them are always evolving, governance must be adaptable. Real Estate, HR, and IT each have distinct methods of updating protocols, implementing change, and communicating information. Governance provides the connective tissue between these three enablement groups, resolving friction points and ensuring that workplace decisions are made collectively, not as individual functions.

As a result, governance structures should also define escalation paths for cross-functional decision-making. When physical, digital, and cultural systems present conflicting priorities, clear criteria and

P

an agreed-upon decision framework prevent deadlock and ensure workplace integrity is preserved.

In addition to aligning the workplace with the organization's behaviors and needs, establish regular review cycles to maintain alignment among these enablement groups. In addition to scheduled reviews, build in proactive triggers for governance reassessment, such as technology rollouts, organizational restructures, new policy launches, or shifts in employee sentiment and behavior surfaced through listening mechanisms. Establishing such thresholds ensures the workplace evolves in lockstep with organizational change, rather than lags behind it.

Like Knowledge Base upkeep, these cycles should be both scheduled and responsive. In this way, Norm Owners and Change Champion networks play a key role in identifying early signs of misalignment and triggering reevaluation before issues escalate.

In addition to scheduled reviews, build in proactive triggers for governance reassessment exercises. Proactive triggers can include technology rollouts, organizational restructures, new policy launches, or shifts in employee sentiment or behavior. Noting and naming these events within your organization's broader ecosystem ensures the workplace evolves in lockstep with organizational change, rather than lagging behind it.

Above all, governance sustains methodological rigor while enabling contextual flexibility. It ensures that your workplace systems—physical, digital, and experiential—continue to function in concert and adapt together, rather than drift apart. When governance is strong, positioning is a sustainable process for keeping work and place in sync.

You'll know your positioning efforts are successful when assessments reveal actionable patterns instead of scattered observations. Rather than disconnected inputs such as, "Meeting rooms are too small" or "People feel disconnected," you'll identify cross-system themes like "Collaboration spaces lack the right technology" or "Communication tools undermine our norms."

Teams should be able to explain how their environment supports or hinders the behaviors defined in your Knowledge Base, generating insights that clarify, rather than complicate your next steps. Instead of accumulating a backlog of isolated issues, Position enables strategic prioritization across functions.

This phase should feel investigative, not prescriptive. The goal is to uncover how environments shape behavior, rather than validate assumptions. Teams often surface unexpected amplifiers and overlooked inhibitors, deepening their understanding of what truly helps or hinders effective work.

Just as importantly, Position normalizes measurement strategies that enable future enablement teams to track the relationship between environment and behavior over time. It clarifies where change is needed, where it is feasible, and where it will have the greatest impact, transforming transformation itself from guesswork into strategy.

P

From Experience

Return to Culture by Way of RTO

In 2022, a client in the technology industry implemented a three-day-per-week Return to Office mandate. Within a month, compliance dropped below 40 percent, rendering the policy functionally obsolete. When the client came to us for help, we began with the following questions:

- Where did things go amiss?

- What was missing?

- How can we right these wrongs and design the right workplace strategy?

P

Our research discovered that the mandate was introduced into an already unstable company culture. In the months preceding our work with them, several executives had left the organization, an employee relations class-action lawsuit had been filed, and a substantial group of new hires had been brought on, despite shifts in revenue. These disruptions created a sense of internal instability, making the sudden Return to Office directive feel like just another destabilizing, poorly researched initiative that was misaligned with employee sentiment and operational realities. It was also assumed that those employed before 2020 would value the office the same way they did before remote work; they didn't.

Adding to the confusion, the company was building more office space but limited access to priority teams. This left 40 percent of employees, mainly those in service functions, without access to physical office space, regardless of preference. With most employees now accustomed to hybrid work, the value proposition for commuting was weak. Alongside the constant change and negative employee sentiment, there was resistance.

Eventually, the data told a different story, and the mandate was replaced with an opt-in model, allowing managers who were closer to the real Employee Experience to determine where their team worked best and how often they would report in person. This shift contributed to early iterations of the **WORK then PLACE** process.

P

We started by reframing the company's workplace decisions around shared purpose. More than half of the workforce had joined remotely and never experienced the culture that the team had fondly remembered pre-2020. We convened a cross-functional group to document two key aspects: the culture that long-tenured employees remembered fondly and the brand appeal that drew new talent. The findings were striking. Employees felt proud to work at the company, but disconnected from its values, processes, and expectations.

With this clarity, we identified where in-person presence might meaningfully support cultural principles, including relationship-building, celebrations, and mutual support. We asked:

What team dynamics call for face-to-face time?

Utilize Bruce Tuckman's Forming, Storming, Norming, Performing model of team development to drive a common language that shapes the norms around the aspects of the workplace that support specific tasks and activities *(Tuckman 1965).*

When was the last time a team had fun together or paused to celebrate?

This company provided entertainment, so remembering that work is fun is imperative, and is exceedingly hard to do alone.

How might tenure, loneliness, or unspoken mental health needs influence behavior?

Elements that are hard to discuss or empathize with require recognition *(Harvard University and Ross 2024).*

We developed these thoughts into a training and individually trained over seventy senior leaders and influential team members or Change Champions—about 1 percent of the organization—to participate. Once teams were anchored in shared work objectives, leaders crafted purpose-driven on-site calendars for each team and developed clearer ways to explain the Why behind each in-person gathering. We then supplied toolkits to guide deeper engagement in areas that can often be deprioritized, including activities for different stages of team development, assessments to evaluate team needs, and ways to identify the need for fun.

After a series of monthly leadership sprints to align on new guide-lines, transparency, and training teams, the revised approach was rolled out to the entire company. But because the mandate aligned with the organization's culture and shared goals, the attrition and engagement challenges were resolved within three months.

What began as a reactive Return to Office effort evolved into a broader cultural transformation. By recalibrating workplace poli-cies to reflect organizational values and strategic goals, leaders gained deeper insights into Employee Experience, enabling a shift toward more sustainable, values-driven change.

- Sara

12

Leverage

Elevating What Works Before Changing What Doesn't

> ## TL;DR
>
> Leverage starts with what already works. It strengthens effective behaviors by making them easier, more visible, and more consistent. Enhancing the good signals progress, builds confidence, and prepares the organization for harder change.

Building on success takes less energy than starting from scratch. That's because it offers quick wins, builds trust, and gives people proof that change can be beneficial, not just disruptive, to their experience.

Leverage is the link between understanding and action. While Position maps what works, Leverage turns that insight into movement. This phase eases the organization into change by reinforcing effective behaviors before addressing what needs to be changed. It builds momentum not by overhauling systems, but by proving that small, strategic improvements can drive meaningful shifts.

Leverage enhances familiar systems, minimizing disruption and increasing return. When employees see meaningful improvements in tools, spaces, or practices they already value, they become advocates for broader change. This optimizes your resources; instead of heavy new investments, you get more from what you already have.

Leveraging Your Workplace Ecosystem

Leverage begins with precision improvements rooted in behavioral insight. The goal is to strengthen what already works across physical, digital, and experiential systems, while ensuring that these improvements reinforce each other rather than compete. This systems-wide perspective builds on the behavioral clarity surfaced during Position and ensures your improvements land where they matter most.

Physical Spaces: Building on What Works

Leverage transforms insights from Position into concrete space improvements that amplify their behavioral impact.

Physical space Leverage often involves modest investments that yield significant behavioral improvements. Examples include improving lighting in areas where teams consistently gather for creative work, adding appropriate technology to meeting rooms that facilitate good decision-making, or creating clearer wayfinding to help people discover underutilized spaces that Position identified as having potential.

L

For example, Position might reveal that phone booths are used for focused work due to high noise levels in open-plan areas. Rather than considering this misuse, Leverage sees this as a signal. Adressing this can look like improving acoustic conditions, creating designated quiet zones, or better communicating which spaces support which work modes.

Digital Tools: Making Good Tools Great

Enhancing digital tools that already align with behavioral norms can include streamlining project management workflows, integrating platforms to facilitate better information flow, or improving the user interfaces of platforms that support asynchronous work.

You may also find integration opportunities across digital tools. For instance, connecting your project planning platform with collaboration or messaging tools to streamline workflows. These improvements typically deliver high impact with relatively low investment and keep your systems aligned with how teams work.

Experiential Systems: Amplifying Cultural Assets

Policy and culture are often your highest-impact Leverage points. Here, Leverage efforts might formalize successful informal practices, replicate effective policies across other teams, or improve how these practices are communicated.

For instance, if a team's lightweight meeting protocols consistently improve collaboration, document and distribute these through your onboarding process. If certain recognition practices support a culture of peer accountability, consider embedding them into performance processes or rituals.

Experiential Leverage delivers strong behavioral returns with low infrastructure investment and authentic pilots. It is the key to normalizing simplified, aligned behavior across your culture.

Leverage strengthens the systems you already have, extending the value of prior investments while minimizing disruption to employees. Its improvements are grounded in behavioral data, not trends or noise. Without this alignment, even well-intentioned upgrades risk becoming vanity projects by being costly, distracting, and disconnected from the way work actually happens. Leverage only what is proven to work. By focusing on targeted, evidence-based improvements, your organization can build a workplace that evolves with purpose and impact.

L

The Four Leverage Actions

To operationalize behavioral insights, the Leverage phase uses four targeted actions: Enhancement, Expansion, Integration, and Optimization. Each action addresses a different opportunity surfaced during the Position phase. These actions can be applied across physical, digital, and experiential systems—but how they're sequenced, resourced, and experienced will vary depending on context. Together, they provide a structured, high-impact path to making what already works even more effective.

Enhancement: Making Good Things Better

Enhancement strengthens effective behaviors by removing friction or amplifying impact through targeted upgrades. If Position revealed that certain meeting rooms consistently support better collaboration, enhancement might mean improving technology, adding more collaborative tools, or offering catering for all-day workshops.

The key principle is to preserve what makes these assets successful while upgrading features or extending their utility. For instance, if employees gravitate toward specific focus spaces but struggle with lighting or ergonomics, introduce higher-quality seating or task lighting. If a digital platform drives accountability but its interface causes friction, redesign workflows or reconfigure settings to streamline usage.

Enhancement involves moderate investment and is ideal for high-use systems where functionality can be deepened.

Expansion: Scaling What Works

Expansion brings proven behavioral amplifiers to broader populations. It identifies practices, tools, or spaces that work well for a specific group and adapts them to support similar needs elsewhere in the organization.

If Position showed that one team's approach to asynchronous collaboration improves delivery speed, expansion might involve coaching other teams on those workflows or adapting the structure for different functions. If a certain room layout enhances brainstorming, replicate its principles across other locations, not just in equal design but also in the behavioral intent behind it.

Expansion is not a copy-paste approach. It requires a contextual understanding of why something works and how it can be translated responsibly. The goal is to scale with integrity—broadening impact while respecting team-specific realities.

Integration: Connecting Isolated Wins

Integration links effective but fragmented solutions within your organization into a more cohesive system. When Position reveals multiple successful tools, spaces, or norms that operate independently, integration connects them to strengthen behavioral flow.

For instance, if your project management software supports transparency and your meeting rooms foster strong collaboration, integration could involve aligning scheduling, tooling, and team norms so these assets reinforce one another. If different departments developed unique, effective training protocols, integration might standardize the underlying principles into a shared onboarding experience.

Integration helps amplify the effect of existing amplifiers by aligning their purpose and usage across teams and environments, reducing redundancy, and creating seamless behavioral support.

Optimization: Maximizing Current Impact

Optimization boosts the usability and efficiency of existing workplace assets without requiring physical or functional changes. It focuses on light-touch interventions that remove minor barriers to adoption or performance.

When Position exercises reveal underutilized breakout spaces that align with your company's collaboration norms, Optimization might involve adding signage, simplifying the reservation process, or re-communicating how they support work aspects. If a useful tool exists but lacks visibility, highlight it in materials or offer brief training refreshers to increase its visibility and awareness.

Optimization is especially powerful in low-cost, high-impact situations where awareness or minor friction is the primary barrier to improvement. These changes are about refining and reinforcing—not redesigning—to ensure existing amplifiers fulfill their potential with minimal disruption.

ENHANCEMENT
Strengthen what works
with modest upgrades

EXPANSION
Scale what works to new
contexts

INTEGRATION
Link successes across
systems and teams

OPTIMIZATION
Refine or reimagine what
is underutilized

L

Together, these four actions create a go-to toolkit for strengthening effective workplace behaviors without overhauling your systems. When applied thoughtfully and in coordination, they help your organization scale what works, reduce friction, and generate visible momentum—all while staying grounded in behavioral evidence. This approach sets the stage for the deeper transformations that follow in Adapt.

Turning Strategy into Action

Identifying the right enhancements is only half the challenge—executing them well is what makes Leverage successful. The following section outlines how to prioritize, coordinate, and communicate improvements across your organization to ensure changes are visible, meaningful, and grounded in shared behavioral goals.

Treat these improvements as structured interventions with clear hypotheses about behavioral impact. This allows your teams to validate effectiveness, adjust quickly, and scale only what works.

Choosing Where to Focus

Start by prioritizing Leverage actions with a broad reach. What amplifiers support multiple behavioral types—such as collaboration, focus, asynchronous work, or socializing—and multiple teams? Choose actions that touch the most people and processes first.

Ask:

- How many people currently benefit from this amplifier?

- How many more could benefit if improvements were made?

- Does it support universal or niche behaviors?

- Will it create visible wins that build momentum?

Space changes may require more coordination and cost, so begin with targeted updates that scale easily. Digital and experiential optimizations often yield high returns for lower effort. Mapping your options against an Impact/Effort map will help guide you in determining which investments will deliver the greatest benefit.

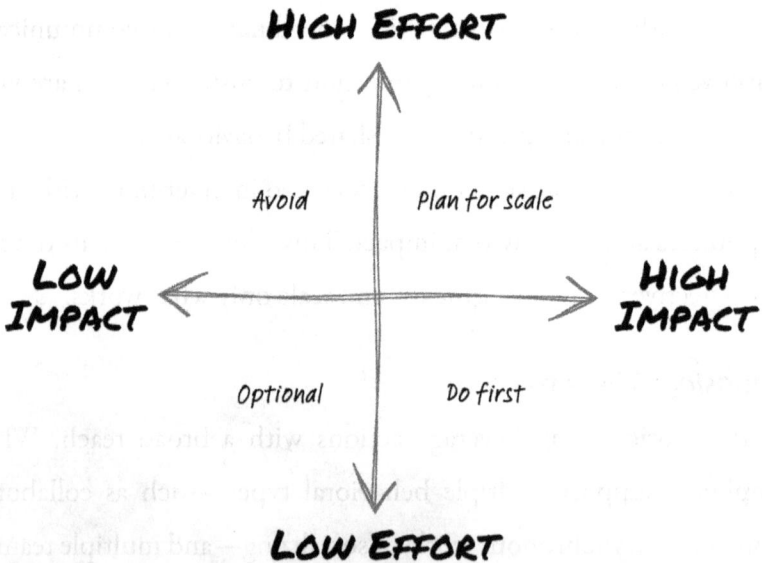

L

HIGH EFFORT

Avoid   *Plan for scale*

LOW IMPACT ← → **HIGH IMPACT**

Optional   *Do first*

LOW EFFORT

Managing Visibility and Expectations

Leverage is visible, and improvements spark comparison. When one team benefits, others may ask, "Where are ours?"

Set expectations by intentionally sequencing improvements. For example, where only targeted enhancements are feasible, explain the behavioral rationale and provide a preview of what a broader application might entail. Avoid creating the perception of favoritism by anchoring communications in shared norms and strategic sequencing, not team-level preferences.

Team Collaboration

Leverage requires an integrated effort across HR, IT, Real Estate, Operations, and possibly other departments. Establish shared goals rooted in behavior, not departmental ownership, and clear protocols for resource allocation, decision-making, and impact evaluation. Improvements should be assessed based on behavioral outcomes, not just functional outputs.

L

This alignment keeps the focus on enabling behavior, not on which team supposedly owns the tool, space, or process. When teams align around shared behavioral outcomes, Leverage becomes the mechanism that transforms strategic insight into practical, organization-wide improvement.

Effective Leverage depends as much on execution as it does on insight. By deliberately sequencing improvements, coordinating cross-functional efforts, and staying grounded in behavioral data, organizations avoid surface-level fixes and drive real progress. The next section outlines how to measure that progress and how to use those results to build confidence for what's next.

Evidence of Effectiveness

Leveraging success should be measured by how much it strengthens core behaviors beyond increased usage or adoption rates. While enhanced resources should see increased usage, the critical question is whether these improvements truly strengthen the documented behavioral norms identified in your Knowledge Base.

Establish measurement approaches that link Leverage investments to behavioral indicators. If Position showed that certain spaces consistently foster effective collaboration, measure whether enhancements to these spaces improve the quality of collaboration, not just booking frequency. If digital tool Optimization aims to support asynchronous decision-making, it should track the speed and quality of decisions, rather than just platform engagement.

Create feedback loops that capture employee experiences with enhanced resources, focusing specifically on how improvements affect their ability to follow documented behavioral norms. This qualitative data provides crucial insight for refining enhancements and identifying additional Leverage opportunities.

Building Confidence for What's Next

Improvements made in Leverage build confidence for the more complex phases ahead. When employees experience meaningful improvements to familiar resources, they become advocates for broader workplace transformation efforts.

Document and communicate your successes to demonstrate the connection between workplace investments and behavioral outcomes. Structure these success stories to clearly link specific Leverage actions to measurable behavioral improvements. For example:

> *"When we [specific enhancement made], employees were able to [behavioral outcome achieved], resulting in [business impact]."*

These concrete examples serve as powerful tools for building support to tackle the more significant challenges that the Adapt phase will address. Use this momentum wisely; it is proof that change, when grounded in evidence, is both possible and welcomed.

Preparing for Adaptation

As Leverage improvements mature, they often reveal workplace barriers that weren't apparent during Position. Enhanced behavioral amplifiers can bring inhibitors into clearer focus, providing valuable intelligence for the next phase of PLACE.

Systematically document these emerging insights, particularly noting where Leverage improvements reach natural limits due to conflicting systems or policies. These constraints often represent the most critical targets for Adapt efforts, as they prevent your optimized behavioral amplifiers from reaching their full potential.

The organizational confidence and cross-functional relationships built during Leverage become invaluable resources for addressing the more complex challenges of transforming workplace inhibitors into behavioral supports.

Articulating effectiveness requires evaluating behavior and sentiment, in addition to utilization and other standard data fields. In doing so, you lay the groundwork for change that is responsive and forward-thinking, rather than reactive and scattered.

Leverage represents the turning point where workplace assessment becomes visible action. Whatever improvements you make during the Leverage phase, validate the organization's ability to evolve with purpose by reinforcing effective practices, demonstrating measurable results, and setting the stage for deeper transformation. As these amplifiers reach their natural limits, they illuminate what still inhibits progress, making the transition into Adapt not just necessary, but inevitable.

L

From Experience

Workplace Lemonade from Office Lemons

In the early days of Hulu, our office in Santa Monica, California—previously occupied by comic Chelsea Handler's *Chelsea Lately* show—was a mix of classic office and production space. Fox, one of Hulu's initial owners, had set up the office for the Hulu team ahead of move-in day. The office was...gray. There were cubicles with 6-foot high dividers, clunky, gray-on-gray workstations, and closed-door offices that obscured natural light from most of the space. It was an old, drab office space that didn't feel like ours. A previous tenant's logo splashed across the carpeting only made that feeling tenfold, not to mention that the last tenant was a defunct company.

"The early days" in start-up speak is code for a few things, including "There's no budget for big office changes." Clearing window-line offices to let in more light, investing in new furniture, and replacing the carpet were all out of the question, but we had to do something. Walking with the ghosts of failed companies past is not helpful for any company's morale, let alone a scrappy start-up racing to launch a brand-new product. We decided that a bucket of yellow paint and a screwdriver could help us set the right tone for the right price.

L

We painted most of the office walls megawatt yellow, figuring that it was the best alternative to natural light we could provide. The color was energetic and cheery, bordering on aggressive. Eventually, the walls became a character in the office and a company-wide meme. The Hulu Wall reached the height of its company fame at the first 'Huluween' party, where Sean Chuang won the costume competition dressed as the wall itself, decked out in head-to-toe yellow. We were part of the office, and the office was part of us.

The cubicles were next. Our trusty screwdriver dismantled the high panels and unused overhead file cabinets and put them on the curb for the next trash collection. It was an improvement, but so many people now joked that they worked in a paintball maze. So, we decided to take that notion and run with it. We bought NERF blasters for everyone, and around 4 p.m. on a Friday, the games would begin. In an instant, the drab gray cubicles transformed into bunkers, protecting people from the flurry of darts flying across the office, momentarily breaking everyone free from the start-up grind while inserting the fun we were creating online into our reality.

As for the carpet, we decided to leave the defunct company logo as it was. It reminded us of our scrappiness and practicality, motivating us to achieve what others before us hadn't. Interviewees would often ask about the logo, which gave us a chance to discuss who we are and what we don't want to be. We weren't precious, and this dead logo on the floor reminded us of that every day. By turning behavioral insight into visible progress, Leverage shifted the tone of transformation from conceptual to tangible, from imposed to embraced. This is how change earns its right to continue.

- Sara

L

13

Adapt
Standardizing Solutions While Preserving Flexibility

TL;DR

While earlier phases revealed what works and what doesn't, Adapt is where transformation begins. It's the pivot point where insight turns into infrastructure, removing friction and building the conditions for consistent, supported behavior.

Adapt removes what obstructs effectiveness and transforms recurring workplace barriers into structured, repeatable enablers of behavior, replacing ad hoc fixes with scalable systems. Its strength lies in modularity. Rather than solving each issue in isolation, Adapt builds a shared workplace language that reduces friction without enforcing uniformity.

Systematic Adaptation

When workplace challenges are addressed in isolation, organizations encounter fragmented experiences, duplicated efforts, and a sense of solution fatigue. Teams often end up solving similar problems repeatedly without access to shared tools or a common language. A unified, repeatable approach allows the workplace to transform barriers into behavioral enablers and establishes a framework characterized by three principles for making future decisions:

Versatility

The Adapt phase identifies shared patterns across diverse cases and conditions to extract lessons and establish consistent outcomes without imposing rigid uniformity.

Ownership

Rather than relying on top-down intervention, local teams gain the structure and confidence to lead changes informed by the broader strategy.

Continuity

This phase builds on known systems and behaviors, reducing disruption and increasing the likelihood of adoption.

A

Over time, systematic adaptation strengthens organizational capability. Instead of treating each challenge as a one-off, the organization develops internal expertise in diagnosing and resolving workplace issues by leveraging a shared behavioral foundation.

213

The Kit of Parts Framework

The Kit of Parts framework establishes standardized, scalable workplace solutions across the three ecosystems—physical, digital, and experiential. Each kit converts Position insights about workplace inhibitors into a curated set of components that reduce behavioral friction while reinforcing the norms documented in your Knowledge Base.

Together, these kits convert Position insights into adaptable, right-sized solutions that scale across teams and contexts without losing behavioral integrity, promoting repeatability, ownership, and continuity. These kits include:

Physical Kit of Parts

While The Kit of Parts offers structured options to meet universal needs with consistency, the Physical Kit addresses space-related inhibitors identified during Position. By establishing a ubiquitous core offering for built environments, issues such as ineffective or insufficient areas for focus, underutilized collaboration spaces, or layouts that undermine social connection are systematically addressed, resulting in a more consistent and enhanced baseline experience for employees visiting the space.

Furniture and Equipment Standards

Define commercial-grade furniture solutions that support diverse work modes. Select durable products with regional availability and bulk purchasing discounts, as these often result in cost reductions of

50 percent or more compared to ad hoc sourcing. Limit the options but give enough choice so that teams feel autonomous.

Space Configuration Options

Create layout templates for common work activities, such as collaboration zones with integrated tech, acoustic focus areas, and social hubs that promote informal connection.

Technology Integration

Standardize how physical spaces support digital tools. Ensure consistent tech support aligns with key behaviors in meeting rooms, team spaces, and individual desks.

Digital Kit of Parts

The Digital Kit targets technology-based inhibitors, particularly poorly integrated tools, convoluted workflows, and misaligned platforms. Your Digital Kit should be established based on these three core principles:

A

Connected

Tools must integrate with documented workflows. Workarounds and siloed systems introduce unnecessary friction and should be retired or simplified to prevent this.

Accessible

Employees should be able to access tools and information reliably across devices and locations. Standardize authentication, hardware, and remote protocols to support verified work patterns.

Usable

Tools should reduce complexity, not add to it. Platforms requiring extensive workarounds or training can negate even well-designed workflows.

Experiential Kit of Parts

The Experiential Kit aligns policies, protocols, and culture with norms and validated work patterns, eliminating the contradictions and ambiguities that Position typically uncovers. The Experiential Kit creates standard approaches to common workplace experiences, such as:

Work Mode Support

Codify expectations for key activities, such as collaboration, focus work, and social connection, to clarify how behavior aligns with shared norms.

Space Utilization Guidance

Communicate how different spaces should be utilized, enabling employees to make informed decisions that align with their task needs.

A

Policy Consistency

Standardize protocols across teams and departments to prevent confusion or conflicting messages.

A well-designed Kit of Parts provides structured flexibility, establishing a consistent foundation for behavior while allowing teams to configure environments based on local needs and context. The aim is not to eliminate variation but to make variation intentional.

When 90 percent of common needs are addressed through standardized components, teams gain clarity without sacrificing adaptability. Employees can navigate complex environments without confusion or guesswork, and leaders can ensure that behavioral norms are upheld without prescribing uniform solutions. This approach prevents the unintentional sprawl and inconsistency that surfaces in Position, while also building the organizational muscle for sustained, scalable change.

Implementation Strategy

Adaptation requires coordinated, cross-system action. Unlike Leverage, which improves existing systems, Adapt introduces more substantial modifications that must be carefully sequenced to minimize disruption and maximize behavioral impact.

A

Prioritization and Sequencing

Begin with the most significant behavioral barriers that affect multiple teams or work modes. Resolving broad inhibitors yields the highest organizational return and paves the way for smoother adoption in the future.

When sequencing Adapt initiatives, evaluate:

Impact Scope: *How many employees are affected by this inhibitor?*

Implementation Complexity: *What technical or operational steps are required?*

Resource Requirements: *What investments are needed relative to the potential behavioral benefit?*

Dependencies: *Does this change unlock or depend on other improvements?*

Although they deliver a durable behavioral impact, physical modifications tend to take longer and cost more. On the other hand, digital changes often deploy more quickly but often demand cumbersome integration and support. As a result, unlike the Physical and Digital Kits, experiential shifts may appear simpler because they lack a hardware or software component. However, the intangibility ultimately requires intentional coordination across policies, protocols, and culture for it to succeed.

Cross-Functional Coordination

The partnership forged between Real Estate, HR, and IT must persist through to the Adapt phase. These changes require intentional collaboration among workplace owners to ensure alignment across systems and to avoid siloed decisions. Real Estate and IT must align on physical changes; IT, Security, and UX must coordinate digital improvements; and HR, Operations, and Leadership must guide experiential shifts. All must communicate the same messages.

The governance agreements established in earlier phases enable fast, coordinated decisions and ensure that decisions remain focused on allowing behavior, not preserving legacy ownership.

Managing Organizational Change

Adapt creates visible shifts that will attract attention, foster enthusiasm, and create resistance. Communicate proactively and transparently, similar to how the behavioral pilots were launched and scaled throughout the WORK phases. Link each change to specific norms and expectations from your Knowledge Base and explain how it addresses a known inhibitor.

Start with changes that demonstrate clear, measurable gains. Then share outcomes openly, and use early wins to build momentum and trust for more complex transformations. By grounding communication in behavior-first rationale and real impact, you build credibility and buy-in for the adaptations to come.

Consistency & Sustainability

Adaptation only succeeds when its improvements are enduring. Sustaining impact requires two parallel efforts: maintaining the systems that support new behaviors, and integrating those behaviors into the organizational culture.

Maintaining Standards

Maintenance in the Adapt phase is similar to upkeeping the Knowledge Base and reviewing governance practices. Kits of Parts must be regularly reviewed to ensure that the resources included still support the organization's needs.

Like any system, Kits of Parts requires regular maintenance. Schedule cyclical reviews—quarterly or semiannually—alongside situational updates triggered by policy shifts, reorganizations, or rapid growth. This balance ensures responsiveness without disorder.

Cultural Integration

Behavioral change endures when it's culturally embedded, not externally imposed. Sustained alignment depends on consistent, transparent communication about how each workplace element reinforces your documented norms.

Communication Strategy

Reinforce the purpose behind changes using the multidirectional communication methods outlined in the Operationalize chapter. Combine leadership messaging, peer-driven storytelling, and visual cues to normalize usage and reinforce the intended purpose.

Habit Formation

Research suggests that forming new habits takes, on average, sixty-six days to feel automatic. In a University College London study, some were able to form a new habit in as little as eighteen days, while others needed 254 to fully shift behavior *(Gardner, Lally, and Wardle 2012)*. To reduce friction and solidify new behaviors, consistently provide guidance, reminders, and gentle reinforcement throughout this period.

Feedback Integration

Build structured opportunities for employees to provide input that gauges how they experience changes. Use insights to refine adaptations and identify emerging inhibitors. Treat feedback not as critique but as an engine for continuous improvement.

Building Organizational Capability

The long-term value of Adapt lies in capability, not just compliance. As teams learn to apply the Kit of Parts frameworks and manage behavioral change independently, the organization builds lasting capacity to evolve.

A

Document processes, decision frameworks, and implementation approaches that work. These resources form the foundation for faster, smarter adaptation in the future, reducing reliance on external support and making change an internal competency.

Evaluating Behavioral Impact

Success in the Adapt phase is defined by observable improvements and systems that remove friction and strengthen behavior.

Behavioral Indicator Tracking

Evaluate whether Adapt interventions improve the behavior patterns they're designed to support. If technology friction previously impeded asynchronous collaboration, track whether newly implemented tools accelerate decision-making and increase the quality of outcomes. Focus on behavioral impact, not just tool adoption.

Inhibitor Elimination

Assess whether identified barriers have been meaningfully reduced or eliminated by using a blend of quantitative data—space or tool utilization, workflow speed—and qualitative insights—user feedback, behavioral ease. Look for signals that employees can now perform desired behaviors with less resistance.

Organizational Capability Development

Gauge whether your organization can now apply standardized, repeatable frameworks to future workplace challenges. Success includes not just fixing what's broken today, but also enabling teams to resolve future inhibitors without having to start from scratch.

Develop measurement strategies that explicitly tie Adapt investments to improved behavioral outcomes. These metrics validate past changes and generate momentum and justification for the Catalyze phase that follows.

Adapt marks the most visible transformation in the *WORK then PLACE* process. It converts friction into flow, turning fragmented tools, spaces, and policies into cohesive systems that enable consistent, supported behavior. Through standardized, scalable interventions, Adapt lays the groundwork for future evolution—not by adding complexity, but by building capability. It's the turning point where infrastructure begins to reflect intention, making the workplace a responsive system for effective work today and strategic growth tomorrow.

A

From Experience

Use What You Have

During the research phase of WeWork's headquarters transformation, our team identified a set of persistent behavioral inhibitors that undermined employee effectiveness each day. Despite the space's vibrant visual energy and brand alignment, it lacked the functional environments required for a high-performing workplace. For starters, competition for quiet space was fierce and constant. Phone booths, which were often the only viable option for heads-down work, were occupied 98 percent of the time. To make matters worse, shared norms around space use were inconsistent or nonexistent, and fragmentation across teams, tools, and protocols meant that HQ enabled friction rather than flow.

Our goal was to transform HQ into a living lab and repurpose as much of what already existed as possible. Operating within the company's own Kit of Parts, responsible for outfitting WeWork locations around the world, helped us to transform existing friction points into a repeatable, systems-based solution that could scale. The key was treating the headquarters not as a finished product, but as a living prototype for a new kind of workplace system.

A

We began with physical adaptation. Using WeWork's existing inventory of commercial-grade furniture and finish materials, we reconfigured key areas based on behavioral needs. A noisy sales bullpen was transformed into "The Study," a quiet zone defined less by architecture than by behavioral expectations. Modest upgrades, including carpeting, monitors, and signage, were enough to signal the shift. The result was a noticeable drop in phone booth overuse and a reliable, soon-to-be fan-favorite space for quiet, focused work.

To address the needs for informal collaboration, we repurposed underutilized zones with café tables and soft seating. These small insertions increased capacity for spontaneous interaction—another major behavioral demand—and reduced pressure on formal meeting rooms.

We also digitally integrated Teem, a WeWork-acquired booking tool, into the Employee Experience. This reduced ambiguity around space availability and improved self-sufficiency, demonstrating a Digital Kit of Parts principle: Remove friction and lack of access to resources through visibility and ease.

Notably, the Experiential Kit of Parts evolved through the involvement of the Community Team. At WeWork, the Community Team was heralded as the "special sauce" that differentiated the company from competitors. This was never more true than in HQ culture. They acted as cultural and change stewards, reinforcing shared norms, facilitating behavioral alignment, and offering on-the-ground feedback. Their work made the space adaptive, not static.

Throughout the process, we focused on iterating upon what already existed—repurposing resources, reinforcing shared behaviors, and minimizing disruption. These interventions didn't just address local issues; they laid the groundwork for broader adaptation. Many of the tactics developed at HQ shaped future PoweredByWe client strategies, validating the core principle of Adapt: Strategic transformation doesn't require reinvention—it requires coherence, intentionality, and repeatable systems designed to scale.

- Corinne

A

14

Catalyze

Scaling Change Without Losing the Thread

TL;DR

Catalyze turns the workplace into a platform for evolution. After foundational improvements are made in Adapt, this phase focuses on expanding capabilities through evidence-based customization, distributed innovation, and continuous learning. The goal is not just to maintain alignment, but also to grow stronger with every change that occurs.

After eliminating what obstructs effective behavior, you're no longer fixing or enhancing—you're enabling emergence. Once norms are established and inhibitors removed, the Catalyze phase empowers teams to refine, adapt, and innovate. Success isn't about enforcing new behaviors. Success is about making new ways of being feel natural. When old patterns become uncomfortable, new ones take hold

C

organically. Catalyze supports this shift by anchoring customization in real-world data, rather than preference or politics, creating systems that are not only resilient to change but also strengthened by it.

Evolution doesn't begin with confidence—it starts with the courage to experiment. Catalyze gives your teams the clarity and trust to try, learn, and improve without waiting for permission.

From Stability to Self-Direction

With workplace inhibitors and other barriers removed during the Adapt stage, your workplace can now operate as a platform for growth. Catalyze advances this maturity by converting stability into agility, shifting from resolving issues to developing new capabilities. Instead of fixing what's broken, this phase invites teams to explore what's possible, building systems that learn, adapt, and scale with the organization through the following:

Strategic Flexibility

The organization adapts to emerging opportunities without eroding the behavioral foundations built in previous phases.

Sustained Innovation

Testing and embracing new norms as opportunities arise ensures that the workplace prioritizes insight-backed adaptability, rather than being restricted by preexisting practices.

Iterative Capacity

Teams develop the skills and structures needed to adapt workplace systems as behavioral and organizational changes occur, rather than experiencing frustration and inertia from unaddressed challenges that build up over time.

Together, these capabilities foster agility through structure. Instead of reacting to change with costly redesigns or disruption, Catalyze enables a proactive, continuous evolution—where the workplace grows in sync with the organization it supports.

Balancing What Stays and What Grows

The Kit of Parts introduced in Adapt becomes foundational infrastructure in Catalyze. Here, those components shift from fixes to frameworks, configured intentionally to safeguard integrity while enabling adaptive reuse.

Catalyze succeeds when organizations differentiate between configuration and customization—two distinct yet complementary approaches to workplace evolution. Configuration safeguards foundational systems by defining non-negotiables, while customization enables adaptive changes based on evidence, rather than preference.

Configuration: Protecting Critical Infrastructure

Configuration uses the established Kit of Parts to deliver reliable, behaviorally aligned solutions. It defines the baseline of what must remain consistent to preserve organizational integrity. These foundational systems often operate "below the waterline"—not always visible to users, but essential to structural stability.

Critical configuration areas include:

- Communication Systems (Physical and Experiential)
- Maintenance Systems (Physical, Digital, and Experiential)
- Technology Infrastructure (Digital and Experiential)
- Scheduling and Access Systems (Digital and Experiential)
- Connection to Purpose and Culture (Across All Ecosystems)

Just like a ship with a hole below the waterline of its hull, failure in these areas can quietly destabilize the entire structure. Configuration protects against that risk by standardizing core elements while still allowing flexible application. Depending on their needs, teams may configure their zones with variations of room layouts and functions that differ from the standard, while still fitting within the predefined parameters that a Kit of Parts provides.

Customization: Enabling Strategic Evolution

Divergence from standard workplace solutions is viable, but only when justified by data and aligned with organizational purpose. When unique cases present themselves and align with your organization's or transformation's North Star, they can support adaptive evolution by responding to documented needs, rather than individual preferences or trend-driven novelty.

Strategic customization should:

- Reinforce documented behavioral norms
- Include measurable success criteria and evaluation plans
- Advance long-term organizational capability

Think of retail environments; every element serves the core objective of driving engagement and sales. When your North Star is central to your team's actions, workplace customizations can offer more than just aesthetic differentiation from the norm. They can foster behaviors that enhance effectiveness and cultural alignment, building strategic distinctiveness without compromising coherence.

When combined, configuration and customization prevent organizational drift. Both are essential for adaptive coherence—configuration holds the center, while customization extends the edge.

Investing Where It Counts

Customization decisions must be grounded in rigorous financial analysis to ensure behavioral return on investment. What may appear as a cost-effective solution on the surface often proves to be disproportionately expensive when measured by actual usage and long-term impact.

Consider two examples:

C

Building an On-site Coffee Shop

- Cost: $1 million to build + $10,000 monthly operations
- Serves: 1,000 employees daily
- Annual cost per employee: $263 ($143 for depreciated build cost over 7 years + $120 for operations)

Adding Conference Rooms

- Cost: $300,000 to build
- Serves: 100 employees (limited by location-specific usage patterns)
- Annual cost per employee: $420 (depreciated over 7 years)

Although the conference rooms have a lower upfront cost, they are 60 percent more expensive per user when measured against actual behavioral utility. Workplace investments need to be evaluated by more than just the cost to design or install. Accounting for the behavioral outcomes each investment supports and the return on investment (ROI) attributed to each use creates a more sophisticated analysis that allows teams to pursue changes that offer the greatest benefit to the population they serve.

Before implementing workplace customizations:

- Conduct cost per user and depreciation analyses
- Account for legal, operational, and maintenance implications
- Estimate real usage based on behavior, not theoretical capacity
- Align investment with clear behavioral outcomes

Without this discipline, customized elements risk becoming symbolic rather than strategic. They risk being difficult to scale, expensive to maintain, and easily decoupled from organizational goals. Anchoring decisions in behavioral evidence and financial clarity ensures that customizations contribute lasting value, not just temporary appeal.

Strategic customization is ultimately a form of leadership signaling. Every investment communicates what the organization values, rewards, and expects. Done well, customization reinforces capability development and makes visible the connection between environment and effectiveness.

While financial modeling clarifies what's worth investing in, governance ensures those investments are implemented with consistency, accountability, and behavioral integrity. The bridge from evidence to execution is where customization either reinforces or fragments strategic intent. The next section outlines how to strengthen that bridge.

Leading Change Without Losing Coherence

In Catalyze, governance focuses on building clarity, clear decision boundaries, shared success metrics, and aligned evaluation methods that allow variation without fragmentation. Effective leaders shift their responsibilities from actively directing change in the workplace to ensuring that teams have the necessary resources to succeed within

C

the newly established boundaries. This involves creating conditions for distributed innovation while preserving the core behavioral and strategic integrity of the workplace.

Governance to Balance Control with Creativity

Establish governance protocols that guide and evaluate customization efforts to ensure consistency and effectiveness. These should include:

- Clear thresholds for when teams may request exceptions to standard configurations

- Cost-benefit frameworks tied to documented behavioral outcomes and capability development

- Shared decision-making protocols across Physical, Digital, and Experiential system owners

- Feedback mechanisms that track how frequently spaces and tools are being used and their effectiveness

This structure enables variation while preserving organizational coherence. It helps teams evolve systems without undermining the behavioral integrity established in earlier phases.

Cross-Functional Coordination

Catalyze requires integrated action across departments that typically operate in silos—Real Estate & Facilities, IT, HR, Operations, and senior leadership—yes, we are back to The Daisy. To avoid fragmentation, align these groups around behavioral goals and the methods for measuring them. Shift accountability from functional ownership to shared outcomes. Customization decisions should serve organizational capability, not individual team preferences.

Quality as Strategic Communication

Every Catalyze implementation becomes a proof point. Sloppy execution damages credibility while thoughtful, high-quality deployments build momentum and trust. For instance, a coffee bar with poor service or a new meeting room lacking acoustic privacy not only fails to deliver value but also erodes confidence in future investments. Cost per user skyrockets when tools are underutilized or misaligned.

Quality signals strategic intent, even in resource-constrained environments. It's not about extravagance—it's about fidelity to purpose. High-quality outcomes show that the organization can manage complexity while maintaining alignment.

Governance in Catalyze shifts from controlling change to enabling evolution. By embedding clarity and coordination into everyday decisions, leaders transform governance into an accelerator of capability, rather than a brake on innovation.

Growing into What's Next

C

Catalyze assumes a foundation of functional systems and optimized supports. It now invites the organization to stretch, test new behaviors, reveal edge cases, and refine innovations in context. The goal is not just to support what works, but to evolve how work happens.

Catalyze invites continued experimentation—but not without guardrails. To unlock advanced behavioral capabilities, teams must be allowed to test and evolve their environments without fear of failure or rule-breaking. That requires safe-to-fail conditions: clearly bounded, intentionally structured, and culturally normalized as part of the process of progress. These efforts aren't about perfection; they're about continuous, intelligent learning.

Testing Emergent Behaviors

Pilot new spaces, technologies, or protocols as behavioral experiments and treat them as learning labs to refine future work models using real usage data.

Unlocking Latent Potential

Enable advanced configurations that support edge cases, such as cross-functional teams, experimental workflows, or unaddressed behavioral needs.

Scaling Successful Innovations

When innovations prove effective, extract their underlying principles and scale intentionally. Avoid the trap of isolated excellence—let success become repeatable.

C

Catalyze sets the conditions for self-sustaining, strategic workplace evolution. When customization is disciplined, evidence-based, and behavior-driven, the workplace becomes a dynamic platform for innovation.

By designing experiments with minimal risk and high learning value, organizations build resilience and adaptability into the fabric of workplace strategy. Catalyze succeeds not when every experiment works but when every outcome—positive or not—strengthens the organization's capacity to evolve. Failures become data, adaptations become knowledge, and each iteration lays the groundwork for what comes next.

How You Know You're Ready

You'll know Catalyze is taking root when teams no longer wait for permission to improve the workplace. They act, reflect, and refine based on shared intent instead. These maturity signals reflect a deeper shift from dependent adoption to proactive evolution. They include:

Proactive Innovation

Teams initiate and test new workplace strategies based on behavioral data, rather than relying solely on leadership or enterprise directives.

Localized Scaling

Customizations that prove effective are replicated across departments, guided by shared principles but adapted to local needs.

Upstream Influence

Successful grassroots experiments begin to inform broader policy, infrastructure, or investment decisions.

C

Integrated Learning Loops

Internal case studies and retrospectives refine future workplace initiatives, reinforcing a culture of evidence-based improvement.

Behavioral Integrity Under Pressure

Even during periods of disruption or urgency, teams maintain alignment with core behavioral norms instead of reverting to legacy defaults.

These signals demonstrate that Catalyze is working not only as a phase but as a competency with an ongoing capability for thoughtful, responsive evolution.

How You Know It's Working

Catalyze success isn't about the number of new features or completed projects. Rather, it's about whether your organization can evolve workplace systems in ways that sustain and strengthen effective behavior over time.

Indicators of Evolutionary Capacity

Track how well the organization adapts its workplace environment without losing alignment to its behavioral foundations. Key indicators include:

- Adoption of newly enabled behaviors that were previously unsupported

- Volume and quality of innovations emerging from improved workplace capabilities

- Team autonomy in making localized adaptations without compromising shared norms

- Organizational agility in addressing new challenges using internal tools and processes

These markers indicate whether Catalyze has established a workplace ecosystem that can absorb change and influence it to grow stronger.

Behavioral Impact Integration

Catalyzing investments must be evaluated by their impact on behavior, not just activity. If a customization is designed to foster deeper collaboration, measure the speed, quality, and inclusivity of collaborative outcomes, not just space utilization or platform logins.

Establish feedback loops that surface employees experience with advanced capabilities. Focus on how these improvements help people engage in the behaviors your transformation aimed to support. This qualitative data provides depth to your quantitative measures and helps refine future investments. Key pieces of any given change may be positive, while others require refinement; the goal is to foster cross-company willingness to approach either openly.

C

Building Systematic Capability

Finally, assess whether your organization can evolve independently. Has Catalyze built the internal capacity to adapt workplace systems without relying on consultants or ad hoc solutions?

Document successful strategies and decision protocols developed during this phase. These become assets for future evolution by accelerating decision-making, reducing costs, and increasing organizational confidence in navigating change. The more your systems evolve with clarity and consistency, the more antifragile your workplace becomes.

Catalyze represents the culmination of the PLACE framework—the point at which your workplace shifts from a static environment to an adaptive system capable of ongoing evolution. By embedding structures for strategic configuration and deliberate customization, this phase enables the organization to respond to change while maintaining its behavioral foundation.

The investments made during Catalyze reposition the workplace as a strategic enabler of agility. No longer reactive or fragmented, your systems now support growth, experimentation, and innovation without eroding what already works. This is the hallmark of a generative ecosystem; one that continually renews its relevance while deepening its coherence.

Catalyze marks the point where your workplace becomes a platform, not a product—an integrated system designed not just to function, but to evolve. When configuration protects what matters and customization enables thoughtful adaptation, the workplace becomes a driver of organizational agility. The investments made during Catalyze don't just support today's needs—they build the capability to meet tomorrow's, ensuring that innovation scales, resilience deepens, and the environment grows with the work it was designed to serve.

When evolution becomes part of how the workplace works—not just what it looks like—Catalyze has done its job.

C

From Experience

Hiding in Plain Sight

As the first in-house workplace strategist for a major commercial landlord in New York City, my role centered on surfacing strategic value from a portfolio of underutilized conferencing, collaboration, and event spaces.

Despite their design quality, these shared environments remained underutilized, not due to physical shortcomings, but because they weren't integrated into tenant workflows. Tenants saw them not as extensions of their workplace, but as adjacent amenities—available but disconnected from purpose.

So, rather than investing in aesthetic upgrades or new construction, we took a catalytic approach: treating existing assets as strategic platforms for tenant capability building. The goal wasn't to retrofit rooms, but to reframe them as enablers of advanced behaviors that tenants couldn't support within their leased footprint.

A flagship building provided early proof of concept. One anchor tenant had long utilized the on-site conference center for its annual shareholder meetings, an event that required scale and elevated support, visibility, and technical infrastructure beyond what was available at their main office. This use case demonstrated how shared spaces could enable high-impact behaviors when activated intentionally.

From that insight, we built a repeatable model. We audited the portfolio, identified similar opportunities, and developed a system-wide strategy for activating shared assets as behavioral infrastructure. These environments became living extensions of tenant strategies, instead of isolated real estate amenities.

We then launched a programming and experience team not just to fill rooms, but to facilitate evolution. Their mandate was to curate events that tested collaboration models, fostered community, and introduced new work modes. Feedback from each activation informed continuous refinement. Over time, tenants began treating these shared environments as part of their internal ecosystem—a modular capability layer rather than an external resource.

To ensure consistency without rigidity, we implemented governance structures, including access protocols, cost-benefit frameworks tied to behavioral impact, and coordination channels between tenant leads, property teams, and operations. This created a scalable system that allowed on-site teams to localize their approach while remaining aligned with a broader portfolio strategy.

C

Overall, the value was clear. Tenants gained flexible, high-performance environments without operational burden, and we avoided capital-intensive build-outs by transforming the portfolio's existing assets into marketplace offerings, enabling behaviors that standard leases couldn't support in their own spaces, and demonstrating that evolutionary capability depends more on stewardship and intention than on investment alone. Most importantly, in the pivotal post-COVID period, we shifted from being a static landlord to a strategic partner in workplace evolution.

– Corinne

C

15

Evolve

Keeping The Workplace's Living Systems Alive

TL;DR

Evolve ensures your transformation doesn't stagnate. It embeds the systems and habits needed for regular reassessment, refinement, and renewal. Rather than reacting to disruption, you build the capacity for deliberate, continuous evolution.

Change never ends—but it can mature. Many transformations launch successfully, only to falter in maintenance. While Catalyze expands your workplace's capacity for adaptability, Evolve sustains it. This final phase of the *WORK then PLACE* process ensures your systems remain aligned as your organization grows, adapts, and learns. Rather than defaulting to reinvention in moments of strain, Evolve embeds the habits and infrastructure needed for ongoing calibration.

This final phase shifts the question from "How do we build the right environment?" to "How do we keep it working as conditions shift?" The answer lies in treating your workplace as a living system with evolving capacity, not a static project.

Turning the Workplace into a Living System

Most transformations don't fail in their design; they fail in their ability to adapt. Without structured mechanisms for ongoing improvement, even expertly designed workplaces fall out of alignment with an organization and a workforce's needs over time. That's because as teams grow, roles shift, and external pressures evolve, static solutions no longer suffice.

Evolve addresses this by embedding continuous improvement into daily operations. To keep pace with the evolution of modern work, occasional workplace transformation must give way to continuous improvement and become a core organizational capability. Thus, instead of rebuilding from scratch, make small, purposeful adjustments that keep pace with organizational change.

This shift brings three essential benefits:

Sustained Effectiveness

Spaces, tools, and culture align continuously with how people work, even as your organization expands and market conditions change. As a result, instead of watching well-designed environments gradually lose their impact, you maintain their effectiveness over time.

E

Reduced Disruption

Smaller, targeted updates that are issued more frequently eliminate the need for major overhauls.

Organizational Fluency

Teams build internal capacity to simplify management and improvement of systems over time, so no external catalyst is required.

The result is a workplace that adapts with you, maintaining alignment with behavior while reinforcing your ability to change deliberately.

How the Workplace Learns

Evolve functions through four interconnected capabilities that keep workplace systems aligned with how people work: Monitoring, Maintenance, Response, and Renewal. These are the vital signs of a healthy workplace system.

Monitoring: Staying Connected to Reality

Monitoring is more than dashboards or data reports. While usage metrics show how systems operate, only employee feedback reveals whether those systems truly support the behaviors documented in your Knowledge Base.

Listen to How People Experience Work

Use consistent feedback methods—such as pulse surveys, focus groups, and informal check-ins—to surface emerging patterns and pinpoint misalignments between systems and actual needs.

E

Watch for Drift

Look for signs where established norms begin to erode due to system friction or changing conditions. Identifying these issues early enables you to make minor adjustments rather than wait for major overhauls later. Pay attention to subtle signals, such as meeting rooms that frequently run over time, collaboration tools that teams stop using, or informal workarounds that bypass official processes.

Focus on Understanding, Not Policing

Monitoring isn't about compliance, it's about system health. Look for areas where the environment fosters good behavior and where small adjustments could help restore alignment.

Maintenance: Preserving What Works

Maintenance in Evolve means sustaining alignment between environment and behavior, not just ensuring things work on paper.

Look Beyond Functionality

Pay attention to the places, tools, and norms that people gravitate toward—the ones they return to out of choice, not necessity. Technical functionality is only one measure of success. Elements that bring lightness, ease, and even enjoyment into the workday are just as important.

E

Keep Physical Spaces Aligned

Adjust layouts, furniture, and equipment as team sizes, work rhythms, and hybrid patterns shift. These are small updates with outsized behavioral impact.

Keep Digital Tools Current

Evaluate updates and integrations through a behavioral lens. Some upgrades improve alignment; others introduce friction. Maintenance sometimes means saying no to change.

Preserve Cultural Practices

Update norms, rituals, and onboarding materials to reflect how work happens today, not just how it was once defined. Reinforce behaviors without adding bureaucracy.

Response: Adapting with Intention

Disruption is inevitable. Growth, turnover, market shifts, and new technologies will test your workplace system. Evolve equips you to respond deliberately, not reactively.

Diagnose Before Acting

Use your established frameworks to assess where systems are stressed and where they still hold. Not everything breaks at once, and not everything needs to be fixed.

E

Leverage Your Toolkit

Reuse the principles and methods from earlier *WORK then PLACE* phases. When anchored in an established strategy, adaptation becomes faster and more consistent.

Document and Learn

Every intervention should produce insight. Track what was done, why, and what outcomes followed. These experiences strengthen your organizational resilience and expand your living Knowledge Base.

Renewal: Strategic Evolution

No workplace element should last forever—not even the ones that once worked well. Renewal ensures that your systems evolve in tandem with your organization's goals and behaviors.

Follow a Schedule, Not a Crisis

Don't wait for failure to justify a review. Build regular refresh cycles into your operations to ensure ongoing effectiveness and efficiency. This reduces risk and prevents complacency.

Preserve Continuity While Enabling Change

You're not starting over, you're evolving what already works to support what comes next. This preserves your organization's accumulated behavioral wisdom while expanding its capacity for change.

E

While continuous improvements are ideal, systems can drift or accumulate misalignment that necessitates a more significant reset. Strategic renewal includes clearing complexity, retiring outdated frameworks, or re-establishing shared baselines. These reboots aren't failures—they're signs of maturity and responsiveness when incremental change no longer suffices.

Together, Monitoring, Maintenance, Response, and Renewal form the operational core of Evolve. These capabilities ensure that your workplace doesn't just support today's behaviors but adapts to tomorrow's. By embedding them into daily operations, your transformation becomes self-sustaining—guided by real needs, shaped by real experiences, and built to last.

Stewarding Change Over Time

Governance in Evolve extends beyond implementation frameworks, becoming a living entity that guides continuity, responsiveness, and cultural coherence without centralized control. Earlier phases built the structures for coordination; now, those structures must become self-sustaining habits. This phase assesses whether distributed decision-making, shared ownership, and feedback integration are consistently practiced.

Sustained transformation requires management structures that strike a balance between coordination and adaptability. Unlike traditional governance models built on top-down control, Evolve

E

supports distributed decision-making guided by shared principles, clear protocols, and mutual accountability.

Set Decision-Making Boundaries With Intention

Distinguish between systemic decisions that affect foundational workplace elements and localized choices that teams can make. Core infrastructure, such as security standards, scheduling systems, and cross-functional workflows, requires centralized oversight to maintain coherence. While local adaptations, like desk arrangements, communication rituals, or work zone configurations, should be owned by those closest to the work. This balance preserves system integrity while fostering responsiveness.

Coordinate Across the Whole Workplace Ecosystem

Workplace systems are deeply interdependent. A new collaboration tool doesn't just change digital workflows—it can shift communication expectations and impact physical space usage. Similarly, reconfiguring a workspace influences cultural dynamics and digital interactions. Governance should ensure that changes in one domain are understood and supported in others.

Make Feedback Actionable and Systematic

Establish reliable channels for employees to share feedback, both through structured tools like pulse surveys and retrospectives, and ongoing behavioral observation. Create processes for synthesizing this input, identifying patterns, and prioritizing adjustments. Feedback isn't a burden to manage—it's insight that keeps the system healthy.

E

Communicate Clearly, Consistently, and Transparently

When workplace changes are explained—what's happening, why it matters, and how they support shared behavioral norms—employees are more likely to engage and participate. Transparent communication fosters trust and signals that the workplace is a dynamic, living system in which everyone contributes to shaping it.

Is This Thing Still On?

Success in Evolve is measured by sustained behavioral alignment, system resilience, and adaptive capability; not by project completion or the rollout of new features. The key indicators reflect system health, not just activity.

Are Your Behaviors Enduring?

Monitor whether core work behaviors identified in your Knowledge Base continue to occur at the right frequency and quality. Are collaboration patterns holding? Are work modes aligning with the spaces and tools designed to support them?

Can Your Systems Flex Without Friction?

Track how effectively your workplace systems adapt to new conditions. Measure both the speed and the success of adaptations. A fast response that fails indicates weak processes; a slow one that works suggests the need for better capacity. The goal is agility with integrity.

E

Is Your Organization Learning?

Evaluate whether your internal teams are becoming more proficient at managing workplace evolution. Reduced reliance on external resources and autonomous adaptations signal growing capability and maturity.

Do Your Systems Still Work Together?

Assess the ongoing alignment of your physical, digital, and experiential systems. Early signs of friction, such as policies undermining tools or spaces that contradict norms, should trigger an investigation. Misalignment is a system health issue, not a one-off glitch.

A Capability, Not A Conclusion

Evolve marks the shift from workplace transformation as a finite initiative to workplace management as a permanent organizational capability. Through *WORK then PLACE,* you've built a system for aligning behavior and an environment that adapts over time.

Your workplace is now a living system—resilient, responsive, and grounded in shared purpose. You have the tools to evolve deliberately, not reactively. While the *WORK then PLACE* framework reaches its formal end, your capacity to support and shape work never stops. With monitoring, maintenance, response, and renewal in place, transformation becomes a continuous practice. The result? A workplace that grows with your organization, not against it.

Completing the Evolve phase creates a sustainable competitive advantage—an organizational capability that enhances effectiveness

E

while minimizing the costs and disruptions typically associated with workplace transformation. You have learned to lead with behavioral insight, demonstrated that systems can adapt without breaking, and built responsiveness into your work infrastructure.

What began as a workplace strategy has evolved into a new way of operating—a blueprint for organizations built to remain effective in the face of continuous change, fostering true transformation. Your workplace is no longer just where work happens; it is how your organization learns, adapts, and thrives. It is both environment and engine—a living system that evolves in tandem with your people, purpose, and priorities.

The journey through What/Why, Operationalize, Regulate, Knowledge Base, Position, Leverage, Adapt, Catalyze, and Evolve doesn't just deliver a better workplace—it builds a smarter organization. What began as a strategy becomes an ongoing capability. Your workplace is no longer just where work happens—it's how your organization learns, adapts, and leads. It's not the end of transformation—it's the beginning of fluency.

Five years from now, you won't need to remember what phase you're in. You'll be using a workplace system designed to grow with and change with your business, shaped by behaviors and strategy, refined by use, and responsive by design—just as it should be.

E

From Experience

Won't You Be My Neighbor?

Following the 2008 financial crisis, many large companies sought to optimize their real estate portfolios while adapting to shifting expectations around flexibility and efficiency. American Express was one of them.

Their response was BlueWork, a workplace strategy that intentionally united physical environments, digital tools, and behavioral expectations. Offices with the BlueWork design featured shared and unassigned seating, a mix of collaborative zones, and a digital booking system that allowed employees to reserve desks as needed. Together, these components formed a cohesive ecosystem designed to support a distributed workforce and reduce underutilized space.

At first, it worked. Utilization data showed promising adjustments, teams adapted, and the balance between real estate efficiency and employee autonomy appeared well-calibrated. But, within two years, deeper issues surfaced—ones the data alone couldn't explain.

Employees began reporting stress around finding seats. Some set alarms to reserve desks as soon as the system opened, and a few even built bots to game the booking process. What was meant to promote transparency and flexibility had instead

E

created scarcity and competition. While the infrastructure remained sound, the behavioral experience had drifted from its intended norms.

Rather than launching a full redesign, the team took a more nuanced approach and targeted renewal through diagnostic listening and collaborative adjustments. Cross-functional retrospectives, employee interviews, and behavioral diagnostics revealed a critical insight: The problem wasn't physical or digital, but relational. The booking tool wasn't broken—it had undermined trust.

With that clarity, the team introduced team neighborhoods to reorganize the space without making any design changes. These zones offered predictable proximity to colleagues while preserving access to collaborative areas and shared spaces. Employees no longer had to compete for desks, nor sacrifice flexibility to gain consistency.

Equally important was how the shift happened. The transition was co-created through open communication and shared governance. Employees weren't just informed of the change—they helped shape it. The workplace didn't just evolve in layout—it evolved in meaning.

Ongoing governance ensured alignment, and feedback loops facilitated the integration of adjustments into practice. The organization didn't wait for a crisis to rebuild trust. Instead, it

E

acted early, using light-touch interventions to maintain system credibility.

The enduring insight wasn't that BlueWork needed to be perfect; it just needed to be tended. Knowledge workers don't require personal ownership of a specific desk—they require belief in the system that supports their work. And belief is built not through novelty or control, but through care, responsiveness, and the quiet reliability of systems that evolve as thoughtfully as the people they serve.

– Corinne

E

Conclusion

Whether or not we are paying attention, our workplaces have always been in conversation with us. Now, more than ever, paying attention to the cues and signals that workplaces give us and taking consistent, informed action is essential for modern work to continue evolving for the better.

When the workplace's digital, physical, and experiential layers operate in harmony, something powerful happens: inertia and friction subside, decisions flow, and trust and engagement build. The workplace becomes a dynamic network of tools, norms, relationships, and spaces that help people focus, collaborate, and contribute to organizational health and effectiveness. What's more, investments that support the holistic wellness of employees and the organization have the potential to unlock nearly $12 trillion in economic value *(McKinsey et al. 2025)*.

However, when these systems operate in isolation, the opposite occurs. Disconnection proliferates, priorities contradict, and people burn out not from working too hard, but from working against the grain of a disjointed system. Although employee productivity is often blamed for workplace dysfunction and disengagement, it is usually a reflection of systemic misalignment that lies far beyond their influence and control. Workplace harmony is possible when expertise from Real Estate & Facilities, HR, IT, and other enablement functions is connected by shared language and collective priorities.

This requires organizations to update their perspectives on work, especially nonlinear and creative knowledge work, as well as the diverse range of behaviors it encompasses. Individual focus, asynchronous coordination, spontaneous collaboration, and even socializing are infrastructures that need to be designed for. No workplace operates in a vacuum. High-performing workplaces in the twenty-first century cannot be treated as separate from employee effectiveness, organizational culture, necessities of life, or broader societal contexts.

By the time this book reaches you, new technologies will have emerged, continuing to reshape how and where work happens. We wrote *WORK then PLACE* to remain useful regardless of the changes that are not yet in our view. The journey and process of change for humans is consistent, regardless of what the change is centered around. *WORK then PLACE* roots into the enduring human experience of change, serving as a reliable guide for workplace transformation long into the future.

WORK then PLACE was designed as a human-centered approach for responding to and integrating change. It deliberately centers the needs of workforces as a conduit for success in this modern era by beginning with behavioral clarity—understanding how people work, codifying what supports them, and testing what doesn't. It then continues with structured experimentation, cross-functional learning, and the evolution of systems that can flex without losing alignment. *WORK then PLACE* helps companies commit to building a new organizational capability and mechanism for change that can be applied to whatever challenge or opportunity arises next, creating conditions for repeatable transformation rather than just one-off wins.

We recognize that there are forces beyond any single company's control—market shifts, labor demands, and technological revolutions. From four-day workweeks to the right to disconnect, organizations will continue to navigate emerging expectations and will need to do so with clarity, transparency, and care. Whether regulated or not, these pressures demand more than policies. They demand thoughtful responses, framed by purpose and centered on people.

Technology, too, is evolving faster than most companies can keep pace with. Tools designed to support work now threaten to replace it. Surveillance systems, such as keystroke logging and passive monitoring, are already in place at many companies, creating further extractive relationships between companies and their employees. This shift toward measurement without meaning and earnest enablement erodes trust and reduces people to mere inputs, rather than collaborators and contributors.

As AI and automation take over more routine tasks, the real work of organizations becomes clearer—to upskill and empower people to do what only humans can do and support the nonlinear, creative, and relational nature that makes humans human. And yet, few companies are investing in human edge. BCG research shows that a mere 14 percent of frontline workers had AI training, versus 44 percent of leaders, further validating that when people are asked to adapt without support, disengagement and quiet resistance follow *(Boston Consulting Group 2023)*. When people are asked to adjust without support, disengagement and quiet resistance follow, destabilizing organizations and creating operational risk in an already volatile market. We cannot expect transformation from a workforce that continues to be under-resourced and unheard.

We believe the next trend, tool, or policy won't define the future of work. Instead, it will be determined by how well companies listen, adapt, and align. The most resilient organizations won't be the ones that get everything right the first time; they'll be the ones that know how to learn—and how to change—deliberately, transparently, and together.

To us, *WORK then PLACE* is a roadmap for how companies can best integrate innovation. We like to say that the workplace is a bit like Rome, because all roads lead to it. Every transformation, no matter where it starts, ultimately returns to the intersection of people, tools, spaces, and behaviors. Integrating strong strategic direction and cultural norms alongside physical and digital ecosystems will be essential to the organizational redesign needed for the future of work.

What we choose to build now will determine whether workplaces become sites of friction or prosperity. And it's the future of work worth building.

References

Accenture. 2025. "Accenture Pulse of Change: Business and Technology Trends." Accenture. https://www.accenture.com/us-en/insights/pulse-of-change.

Accenture, John-Paul Pape, David A. Ramirez, and Elena Pienkowski. 2022. "The Future of Work 2022." Accenture. https://www.accenture.com/us-en/insights/consulting/future-work.

Accenture and Qlik. 2020. "The Human Impact of Data Literacy." Accenture. https://www.accenture.com/content/dam/accenture/final/a-com-migration/r3-3/pdf/pdf-118/accenture-the-human-impact-data-literacy.pdf.

Alation and Wakefield Research. 2021. "State of Data Culture." Alation. https://downloads.ctfassets.net/7p3vnbbznfiw/68xue61hwx5rvKPiTWc6zL/1234ae8f-5504c6ac1bd1eb144afda720/the-alation-state-of-data-culture-report-q2-2021.pdf.

Atlas. 2025. "Exploring the Global 'Right to Disconnect': Shaping Work-Life Balance in 2025." Atlas HXM. https://www.atlashxm.com/resources/global-right-to-disconnect-policies-work-life-balance.

AWA Performance Innovation Network. 2014. "The 6 Factors Of Knowledge Worker Productivity... That Change Everything." Advanced Workplace Associates. https://www.advanced-workplace.com/wp-content/uploads/2015/04/6_Factors_Paper.pdf

Axios and Emily Peck. 2024. "Where Workers Have the 'Right to Disconnect.'" Axios. https://www.axios.com/2024/08/30/world-right-to-disconnect-countries-map.

Basiouny, Angie, and Wharton. 2022. "Can the U.S. Embrace a Four-day Workweek?" Knowledge at Wharton. https://knowledge.wharton.upenn.edu/article/can-the-u-s-embrace-a-four-day-workweek/

Bloom, Nicholas, Jose M. Barrero, Steven Davis, Brent Meyer, and Emil Mihaylov. 2023. "Survey: Remote Work Isn't Going Away—and Executives Know It." *Harvard Business Review*. https://hbr.org/2023/08/survey-remote-work-isnt-going-away-and-executives-know-it.

Bloom, Nicholas, Ruobing Han, and James Liang. 2024. "Hybrid Working from Home Improves Retention Without Damaging Performance." *Nature*. https://www.nature.com/articles/s41586-024-07500-2.

Bloomberg and Sridhar Natarajan. 2021. "Goldman CEO Warns Remote Work Is Aberration, Not the New Normal." *Bloomberg News*. https://www.bloomberg.com/news/articles/2021-02-24/goldman-ceo-warns-remote-work-is-aberration-not-the-new-normal.

Bloomberg News, Mia Gindis, and Matthew Boyle. 2023. "Shopify Doubles Down on Meeting Purge by Shaming Employees with Cost Calculator." *Financial Post*. https://financialpost.com/fp-work/shopify-discourages-meetings-shaming-cost-calculator.

Boston Consulting Group. 2023. "Just 14% of Frontline Employees Have Received Training to Address How AI Will Change Their Jobs, But 86% of Employees Say They'll Need It." Boston Consulting Group. https://www.bcg.com/press/7june2023-frontline-employees-how-ai-will-change-jobs.

Brusati, Isabella, and Prosci. 2024. "Organizational Transformation: What It Is and How To Succeed." Prosci. https://www.prosci.com/blog/organizational-transformation.

Calm Business. 2023. *2023 Workplace Mental Health Trends Report*. Scribd. https://www.scribd.com/document/691007364/Calm-Business-2023-Workplace-Mental-Health-Trends-Report.

CBRE Insights. 2024. *Global Office Fit Out Cost Guide*. CBRE. https://sprcdn-assets.sprinklr.com/2299/73444f59-8d8a-4fee-a857-c32c21e5dc44-610313635.pdf.

Clear, James. 2018. *Atomic Habits: An Easy & Proven Way to Build Good Habits & Break Bad Ones*. New York: Avery.

Deloitte. 2023. "Deloitte Global—2023 Gen Z and Millennial Survey." Deloitte. https://www.deloitte.com/global/en/about/press-room/2023-gen-z-and-millenial-survey.html.

Deloitte, Corrie Commisso, and Sue Cantrell. 2023. "Outcomes Over Outputs: Why measuring productivity is no longer the metric that matters most." Deloitte. https://www.deloitte.com/us/en/insights/topics/talent/measuring-productivity.html.

Deloitte, Jen Fisher, and Alexis Werbeck. 2024. "The Important Role of Leaders in Advancing Human Sustainability." Deloitte. https://www.deloitte.com/us/en/insights/topics/talent/workplace-well-being-research-2024.html.

Deloitte Insights. 2023. "Partially Virtual, Wholly Productive: The Hybrid Culture of Tomorrow." Deloitte. https://www.deloitte.com/us/en/services/consulting/articles/hybrid-culture-transformation.html

Dropbox. n.d. "Virtual First: Effectiveness Kit." Dropbox. https://aem.dropbox.com/cms/content/dam/dropbox/dmep/en-us/assets/pdfs/Virtual_First_Toolkit_Effectiveness_Meetings_101.pdf.

Drucker, Peter. 1959. *Landmarks of Tomorrow*. New York: Harper Brothers. https://archive.org/details/landmarksoftomor0000unse/page/n9/mode/2up.

Dunning, David, and Justin Kruger. 1999. "Dunning-Kruger Effect."

Economic Policy Institute, Aaron Sojourner, and Adam Reich. 2025. "Americans Favor Labor Unions Over Big Business Now More Than Ever." Economic Policy Institute. https://www.epi.org/blog/americans-favor-labor-unions-over-big-business-now-more-than-ever/.

The Economic Times. 2024. "Japan Plans to Give Three Weekly Offs to Everybody From Next Year to Grow Younger." *The Economic Times*. https://economictimes.indiatimes.com/news/international/global-trends/japan-plans-to-give-three-weekly-offs-to-everybody-from-next-year-to-grow-younger/articleshow/116207702.cms?from=mdr.

Edelman. 2025. "2025 Edelman Trust Barometer." Edelman. https://www.edelman.com/trust/2025/trust-barometer.

Federal Reserve Bank of San Francisco. 2024. "Productivity During and Since the Pandemic." Federal Reserve Bank of San Francisco. https://www.frbsf.org/research-and-insights/publications/economic-letter/2024/11/productivity-during-and-since-pandemic/.

Fellow. 2024. *The State of Meetings Report 2024*. Fellow.app. https://fellow.app/resources/state-of-meetings-2024.

Forrester and Phil Harrell. 2020. "A Sales Executive's Perspective on Alignment: Outdated Stereotypes, Pipeline and Revenue Goals for Marketing." Forrester. https://www.forrester.com/blogs/sales-executive-perspective-on-alignment/.

4 Day Week Global. "4 Day Week Pioneering Pilot Program a Huge Success, New Research Reveals." 4 Day Week Global. https://www.4dayweek.com/press-releases-posts/4-day-week-pioneering-pilot-program-a-huge-success-new-research-reveals-ape69.

4 Day Week Global. 2023. "The 4 Day Week UK Results." 4 Day Week Global. https://www.4dayweek.com/uk-pilot-results.

Future Forum. 2021. *Future Forum Pulse: The Great Executive-Employee Disconnect*. Future Forum. https://futureforum.com/research/the-great-executive-employee-disconnect/.

Gardner, Benjamin, Philippa Lally, and Jane Wardle. 2012. "Making Health Habitual: The Psychology of 'Habit-Formation' and General Practice." *British Journal of General Practice* 62, no. 605 (December): 664-666. https://doi.org/10.3399/bjgp12X659466.

GatherFor and Teju Ravilochan. 2021. "Could the Blackfoot Wisdom that Inspired Maslow Guide Us Now?" GatherFor. https://gatherfor.org/blog/blackfoot-influence-on-maslow.

Gopnik, Alison. 2016. *The Gardener and the Carpenter: What the New Science of Child Development Tells Us About the Relationship Between Parents and Children.* New York: Farrar, Straus and Giroux.

Granovetter, Mark, and Johns Hopkins University. 1973. "The Strength of Weak Ties." *American Journal of Sociology* 78, no. 6 (May): 1360-1380. https://www.jstor.org/stable/2776392.

Harvard University and Elizabeth M. Ross. 2024. "What is Causing Our Epidemic of Loneliness and How Can We Fix It?" Harvard Graduate School of Education. https://www.gse.harvard.edu/ideas/usable-knowledge/24/10/what-causing-our-epidemic-loneliness-and-how-can-we-fix-it.

Hofstra Labor & Employment Law and Nancy B. Schess. 2013. "Then and Now: How Technology has Changed the Workplace." Hofstra Labor & Employment Law JournalHofstra Labor & Employment Law Journal. https://scholarlycommons.law.hofstra.edu/cgi/viewcontent.cgi?article=1550&context=hlelj

Hogan, Kathleen, Valerio Pellegrini, and Microsoft. 2021. "Research Proves Your Brain Needs Breaks." Microsoft. https://www.microsoft.com/en-us/worklab/work-trend-index/brain-research.

HP. 2023. *Work Relationship Index.* HP Press. https://press.hp.com/content/dam/sites/garage-press/press/press-kits/2023/hp-work-relationship-index/_HP%20WRI%2023%20Whitepaper%20Report_091923.pdf.

Hudelson, Patricia M. 2004. "Culture and Quality: An anthropological perspective." *International Journal for Quality in Health Care* 16, no. 5 (October): 345–346.

i4cp. 2024. "Future-Proofing Your Organization for Unpredictable Times." i4cp. https://www.i4cp.com/press-releases/future-proofing-your-organization-for-unpredictable-times#:~:text=%E2%80%9CAs%20organizations%20revise%20return,embrace%20change%20and%20quickly%20take.

IBM Education. 2023. "What is a Knowledge Worker and What Do They Do?" IBM. https://www.ibm.com/think/topics/knowledge-worker.

References

International Labour Office, Janine Berg, and Pawel Gmyrek. 2023. *Automation Hits the Knowledge Worker: ChatGPT and the future of work*. United Nations. https://sdgs.un.org/sites/default/files/2023-05/B59%20-%20Berg%20-%20Automation%20hits%20the%20knowledge%20worker%20ChatGPT%20and%20the%20future%20of%20work.pdf.

Iskander, Morkos. 2018. "Burnout, Cognitive Overload, and Metacognition in Medicine." *Medical Science Educator* 29, no. 15 March 2019 (November): 325–328. https://doi.org/10.1007/s40670-018-00654-5.

Kitterman, Ted, and Great Place to Work. 2024. "How Return-to-Office Mandates Pose Risks to Productivity, Well-Being, and Retention." Great Place to Work. https://www.greatplacetowork.com/resources/blog/how-return-to-office-mandates-pose-risks-productivity-wellbeing-retention#:~:text=The%20survey%20shows%20that%20mandates,employee%20retention%2C%20productivity%2C%20and%20more.

Kübler-Ross, Elisabeth. 1969. The Stages of Grief in *On Death and Dying*. London: Routledge.

Lee, Hanju, and Johns Hopkins University. 2022. "The Changing Generational Values." Johns Hopkins University. https://imagine.jhu.edu/blog/2022/11/17/the-changing-generational-values/.

Lovich, Deborah, and Rosie Sargeant. 2023. "Making Flexible Working Models Work." Boston Consulting Group. https://www.bcg.com/publications/2023/flexible-working-models?tpcc=NL_Marketing.

McKinsey. 2021. *Future Proof: Solving the "adaptability paradox" for the long term*. McKinsey & Company. https://www.mckinsey.com/capabilities/people-and-organizational-performance/our-insights/future-proof-solving-the-adaptability-paradox-for-the-long-term.

McKinsey. 2022. *What is industry 4.0 and the Fourth Industrial Revolution?* McKinsey & Company. https://www.mckinsey.com/featured-insights/mckinsey-explainers/what-are-industry-4-0-the-fourth-industrial-revolution-and-4ir.

McKinsey. 2022. *Americans Are Embracing Flexible Work—And They Want More of It.* McKinsey & Company. https://www.mckinsey.com/industries/real-estate/our-insights/americans-are-embracing-flexible-work-and-they-want-more-of-it.

McKinsey. 2023. *The State of Organizations 2023*. McKinsey & Company. https://www.mckinsey.com/~/media/mckinsey/business%20functions/people%20and%20organizational%20performance/our%20insights/the%20state%20of%20organizations%202023/the-state-of-organizations-2023.pdf.

McKinsey. 2023. *What Matters Most? Eight CEO priorities for 2024.* McKinsey & Company. https://www.mckinsey.com/capabilities/strategy-and-corporate-finance/our-insights/what-matters-most-eight-ceo-priorities-for-2024.

McKinsey. 2024. *Healthy Organizations Keep Winning, But the Rules Are Changing Fast.* McKinsey & Company. https://www.mckinsey.com/capabilities/people-and-organizational-performance/our-insights/healthy-organizations-keep-winning-but-the-rules-are-changing-fast.

McKinsey. 2024. "Developing a Resilient, Adaptable Workforce for an Uncertain Future. McKinsey & Company. https://www.mckinsey.com/capabilities/people-and-organizational-performance/our-insights/developing-a-resilient-adaptable-work-force-for-an-uncertain-future.

McKinsey. 2025. "Achieving Growth: Putting leadership mindsets and behaviors into action." McKinsey & Company. https://www.mckinsey.com/capabilities/growth-marketing-and-sales/our-insights/achieving-growth-putting-leadership-mindsets-and-behaviors-into-action.

McKinsey, Wouter Aghina, Karin Ahlback, Aaron De Smet, Gerald Lackey, Michael Lurie, Monica Murarka, and Christopher Handscomb. 2018. *The Five Trademarks of Agile Organizations.* McKinsey & Company. https://www.mckinsey.com/capabilities/people-and-organizational-performance/our-insights/the-five-trademarks-of-agile-organizations.

McKinsey, Aykut Atali, Chandra Gnanasambandam, and Bhargs Srivathsan. 2019. *Transforming Infrastructure Operations for a Hybrid-Cloud World.* McKinsey & Company. https://www.mckinsey.com/~/media/McKinsey/Industries/Technology%20Media%20and%20Telecommunications/High%20Tech/Our%20Insights/Transforming%20infrastructure%20operations%20for%20a%20hybrid%20cloud%20world/Transforming-infrastructure-operations.pdf.

McKinsey, Tessa Basford, and Bill Schaninger. 2016. "The Four Building Blocks of Change." McKinsey & Company. https://www.mckinsey.com/capabilities/people-and-organizational-performance/our-insights/the-four-building-blocks--of-change.

McKinsey, Barbara Jeffery, Brooke Weddle, Jacqueline Brassey, and Shail Thaker. 2025. *Thriving Workplaces: How employers can improve productivity and change lives.* McKinsey & Company. https://www.mckinsey.com/featured-insights/world-economic-forum/knowledge-collaborations/thriving-workplaces-how-employers-can-improve-productivity-and-change-lives.

McKinsey, Erik Schaefer, Joris Wijpkema, and Richard Sellschop. 2024. "Breaking Operational Barriers to Peak Productivity." McKinsey & Company. https://www.mckinsey.com/capabilities/operations/our-insights/breaking-operational-barriers-to-peak-productivity

Microsoft and Ana Galvañ. 2025. *Breaking Down the Infinite Workday*. Microsoft. https://www.microsoft.com/en-us/worklab/work-trend-index/breaking-down-infinite-workday.

MIT Sloan, Álvaro Lleó de Nalda, Alex Montaner, Amy C. Edmondson, and Phil Sotok. 2022. "Unlock the Power of Purpose." *MIT Sloan Management Review*. https://sloanreview.mit.edu/article/unlock-the-power-of-purpose/#:~:text=Companies%20that%20have%20defined%20a,1.

MIT Sloan and Benjamin Laker. 2023. "How Far-Reaching Could the Four-Day Workweek Become?" *MIT Sloan Management Review*. https://sloanreview.mit.edu/article/how-far-reaching-could-the-four-day-workweek-become/#:~:text=The%20world%E2%80%99s%20most%20extensive%20four,in%20absences%20and%20sick%20days.

Monahan, Kelly, Gabby Burlacu, and Upwork. 2024. "From Burnout to Balance: AI-Enhanced Work Models for the Future." Upwork. https://www.upwork.com/research/ai-enhanced-work-models.

National Council of Compensation Insurance and Patrick Coate. 2021. *Remote Work Before, During, and After the Pandemic*. National Council on Compensation Insurance. https://www.ncci.com/SecureDocuments/QEB/QEB_Q4_2020_RemoteWork.html.

The New York Times and Shira Ovide. 2021. "The Big Impact of Small Changes." *The New York Times*. https://www.nytimes.com/2021/06/22/technology/digital-habits.html.

Norton, D.W., Pine II, B.J. 2009. "Unique experiences: disruptive innovations offer customers more 'time well spent'." *Strategy and Leadership*. 37. (6). 4-9.

Oak Engage. 2023. "10 Shocking Workplace Change Statistics for 2023." Oak Engage. https://www.oak.com/blog/10-shocking-workplace-change-statistics-for-2023/#:~:text=Frontline%20employees%20taking%20the%20initiative,%28McKinsey.

Parker, Kim, and Pew Research Center. 2025. "Many Remote Workers Say They'd be Likely to Leave Their Job if They Could No Longer Work From Home." Pew Research Center. https://www.pewresearch.org/short-reads/2025/01/13/many-remote-workers-say-theyd-be-likely-to-leave-their-job-if-they-could-no-longer-work-from-home/.

Pellegrini, Valerio, and Microsoft. 2022. *Great Expectations: Making Hybrid Work Work*. Microsoft. https://www.microsoft.com/en-us/worklab/work-trend-index/great-expectations-making-hybrid-work-work.

271

Perlow, Leslie A., Constance N. Hadley, and Eunice Eun. 2017. "Stop the Meeting Madness." *Harvard Business Review*. https://hbr.org/2017/07/stop-the-meeting-madness.

Prochaska, James, and Carlo DiClemente. 1977. "Transtheoretical Model of Behavior Change."

Prosci. 2024. "Change Agents: Catalysts for Organizational Growth." Prosci. https://www.prosci.com/blog/change-agent.

Rubin, April, and Axios. 2025. "These Major Companies Want Workers Back in the Office." Axios. https://www.axios.com/2025/01/01/back-to-work-office-companies.

Schaffer, Richard H. 2017. "All Management is Change Management." *Harvard Business Review*. https://hbr.org/2017/10/all-management-is-change-management.

Schwab, Klaus. 2017. *The Fourth Industrial Revolution*. New York: Crown Currency.

SHRM Labs. 2024. "Operationalizing Feedback." SHRM Labs. https://www.shrm.org/labs/resources/operationalizing-feedback.

Slack. 2023. "The State of Work in 2023." Slack. https://slack.com/blog/news/state-of-work-2023.

Slack. 2023. "The Surprising Connection Between After-Hours Work and Decreased Productivity." Slack. https://slack.com/blog/news/the-surprising-connection-between-after-hours-work-and-decreased-productivity.

Slack and Brian Elliot. 2022. "Focus Fridays and Maker Weeks at Slack." Slack. https://slack.com/blog/news/focus-fridays-and-maker-weeks-at-slack.

Takano, Congressman Mark. 2023. "Congressman Takano Reintroduces 32 Hour Workweek Act." Mark Takano Congressman for the 39th District of California. https://takano.house.gov/newsroom/press-releases/congressman-takano-reintroduces-32-hour-workweek-act.

Taleb, Nassim N. 2014. *Antifragile: Things That Gain from Disorder*. New York: Random House.

Taylor, Frederick. 1903. "Shop Management." *Transactions of the American Society of Mechanical Engineers* 24 (January): 1337-1456.

TL;DR. ~2002.

Tuckman, Bruce. 1965. "Developmental Sequence in Small Groups." *Psychological Bulletin* 63 (6): 384–399. https://psycnet.apa.org/doiLanding?doi=10.1037%2Fh0022100.

US Department of Labor. 2024. *Trendlines*. US Department of Labor. https://www.dol.gov/sites/dolgov/files/ETA/opder/DASP/Trendlines/posts/2024_08/Trendlines_August_2024.html.

Werbeck, Alexis. 2023. "Hybrid Workers Seek the Best of In-Office and Remote Work." Deloitte. https://www.deloitte.com/us/en/insights/industry/telecommunications/connectivity-mobile-trends-survey/2023/hybrid-work-challenges-statistics.html.

Wigert, Ben, Jim Harter, and Sangeeta Agrawal. 2023. "The Future of the Office Has Arrived: It's Hybrid." Gallup. https://www.gallup.com/workplace/511994/future-office-arrived-hybrid.aspx.

Willamett University. n.d. "Fordism & Postfordism." Willamette University. https://people.willamette.edu/~fthompso/MgmtCon/Fordism_&_Postfordism.html.

WorkLife, Adam Grant, and John Amaechi. 2021. "Building an Anti-Racist Workplace." TED. https://www.ted.com/podcasts/worklife/building-an-anti-racist-workplace-transcript.

World Economic Forum and Gabi Thesing. 2023. "Why Flexible Working is Good for Workers and Companies." World Economic Forum. https://www.weforum.org/stories/2023/01/flexible-working-benefits-ilo-report/#:~:text=Organization%20%28ILO%29%20has%20found.

World Economic Forum, Johnny Wood, and Ian Shine. 2023. "Right to Disconnect: The countries passing laws to stop employees working out of hours." The World Economic Forum. https://www.weforum.org/agenda/2023/02/belgium-right-to-disconnect-from-work/.

Wurman, Richard S. 1989. *Information Anxiety*. New York: Doubleday.

Zenger Folkman. 2022. "8 Unforeseen Rewards for Leaders Who Listen More." Zenger Folkman. https://zengerfolkman.com/articles/8-unforeseen-rewards-for-leaders-who-listen-more/.

Zhao, Nan, Xian Zhang, Adam Noah, Mark Tiede, Joy Hirsch, and Yale University. 2023. "Separable Processes for Live "In-Person" and Live "Zoom-Like" Faces." *Imaging Neuroscience*. https://direct.mit.edu/imag/article/doi/10.1162/imag_a_00027/117875/Separable-processes-for-live-in-person-and-live.

Zoom. 2023. "Survey: Flexible Work Rises As Top Perk." Zoom. https://www.zoom.com/en/resources/survey-workers-want-flexible-work/?cms_guid=false&lang=null.

Corinne's Acknowledgments

I remember when I first heard the phrase "workplace strategy."

I was maybe two years out of college, working as a broker in New York City, and feeling directionless. To help me find my footing, my mentor created an apprenticeship program just for me, connecting me to the many niches within and adjacent to commercial real estate. This helped me begin to see where I might thrive. It would be another two years before I landed my first workplace job, but the advocacy of Dave Florio and Steve Siegel nearly fifteen years ago laid the groundwork for everything that has followed.

Each step on my career path, and the friendships formed along the way, have shaped my worldview on the workplace and the future of work. Anne, Susan, Rachel, Lakshmi, Adam, Kaylie, Matt, Macaulay, Cory, Tom, Phil, Veresh, Lendy, Alex, Jen, and many more lent me their time and wisdom as I nurtured new concepts, sharpening my ideas and gradually turning them into something usable and actionable. In more recent years, members of the Future of Work Alliance have been invaluable sources of inspiration and guidance, encouraging me to keep carving my path at the edge of the future of work.

Compared to peers with degrees in business, architecture, design, and engineering, my background in religious studies has often made me a bit of a wildcard. For years, it just felt like a quirky footnote of my personal history; an interesting tidbit, but unrelated to my professional life. That changed when I got to WeWork.

For all its quirks and flaws, WeWork gave me the space to explore the inner workings of companies—the cultures, behaviors, and rituals that shape them and how to improve them for employees and the business. For the first time, I could draw a clear line between my studies and my work, and I began to fully understand how the lens that my education offered me could unlock in the future.

As AI accelerates and the humanities and interdisciplinary studies become more essential than ever, I find myself appreciating my Gettysburg College education more with each passing year. Professors Stephen Stern, Buz Myers, Megan Sijapati, and Ken Lokensgard helped me to build the intellectual foundation I now draw from constantly. I hope to continue weaving that knowledge into the future of work, because there is still so much more to discover when we look at work through this lens.

Most of the core intellectual influences for *WORK then PLACE* are cited in its pages, except for one. I first read Jenny Odell's *How to Do Nothing* in late 2019, right after leaving WeWork. I was recovering from burnout and wondering what to do next. Odell's work is a rallying cry for readers to reclaim their attention from the distraction economy and redirect it toward presence with the self, others, and spirit—or, in her case, with the birds and trees in her local park.

I felt the truth of her words immediately. But, professionally, I knew that her call to action was easier said than done. Much of what drives people toward distraction and disconnection, especially in the United States, is rooted in our work culture. The instability, unrelenting pace, lack of clarity, and inevitable burnout wear workers down to the point where doing nothing feels impossible and the temptation of distraction is unavoidable. Long before most people could even begin to imagine the kind of presence Odell describes, I knew that real change would require a transformation that makes organizations more effective and less cognitively taxing.

When Sara asked me to be her coauthor, I knew *WORK then PLACE* would be our contribution to that goal; improving organizational outcomes and Employee Experience, while also creating the kind of broader cultural conditions where Odell's wisdom could take root. From the start, I knew writing a book would be a massive undertaking, but the lived experience of writing it was more intense and consuming than I could have imagined. It was all worth it, and I am so grateful that I wasn't in this alone.

Sara's generosity and collaborative spirit made this book possible, and I'm so proud to have been her partner. Our complementary expertise, our East Coast and West Coast contexts, and our shared vision all worked in harmony toward the singular goal of writing the best book we could. I am so grateful to the team at Munn Avenue Press, our editors Holly Hudson and Selah Griffin, who helped us bring our vision to life—transforming what began in our friend Omar's office and deepened during a retreat in Joshua Tree into the book you now read.

This project marked a turning point in my life, and I am enormously grateful to the close friends who walked with me through each step of this journey. Breakfast dates and concerts with C-J. Daily, sometimes day-long, conversations with Shar. Escapes to the woods and into esoterics with Jenny and Ashley (who also designed our cover). And long philosophical, existential, and heartfelt talks with Ben. Their love, care, and encouragement have meant the world to me and remind me of how lucky I am to be surrounded by the best of the best.

Last, but never least, my family. The love and support of my parents have been steady and unconditional throughout my life, but I've felt it more profoundly in these past few years. There will never be enough ways to say thank you.

Despite there being five adults, three (loud) kids, and three (loud) dogs around, my sister and brother-in-law's home was one of my favorite places to write. The proximity to my close family, especially my young nieces and nephews, offered a kind of grounding I didn't know I needed as I wrestled with how to convey our message best. It turns out, being around babies and toddlers makes the future feel far less abstract.

By the time they and their Generations Alpha and Beta peers enter the workforce, many of the struggles we wrestle with today will likely be relics of a different era. That's because the future is always in a constant state of unfolding. And the workplace strategists of tomorrow—and the tomorrow after that—will continue to interpret the needs of organizations and workforces, and find ways to move the needle of progress forward and make work suck just a little bit less.

Sara's Acknowledgments

One of the great things about the partnership with Corinne is that we are different and have complimentary skills. I tend to speak in bullet points and big thoughts, and she makes it all readable and engaging. So this will be the one section that doesn't have "Corinne Magic" added to it.

Thank you to:

Corinne, my amazing coauthor, friend and fellow Workplace nerd.

My mom, Jane, the woman who inspires me to do hard things and enjoy the journey.

My husband, Esco, my forever "Stewie".

My girls, Lauren, Karen, Rita and Gretyl, my reason.

The champions and facilitators of my career - Jim O'Gorman, Rob Waller, Jason Kilar, John Foster, Jill Motaman, and the Pepperdine Rho Prime MSOD professors.

My relentlessly supportive friends, each in their own way, with a special call out to Lindsey Gray who has heard it all as I built my Workplace career (and adult life) and helped it make sense.

My colleagues and teams who create impactful Workplaces every day and ignite Workplace progress. Especially my Hulu WE (Workplace Experience) team who endured through my discovery of Workplace and held up so many of my crazy ideas before I knew how to listen and partner to make crazy ideas even better.

The companies who have put up with and often embraced my search for a better Workplace future—Hulu, Honey, PayPal, Cafe, Netflix, Calm, Riot Games, CBRE, and more.

Those who helped this book reach the world, especially the Munn team, Holly, Selah and Ashley who all gave us exceptional patience, kindness, and care.

Last, but not least, thanks to YOU, the reader. I love what I do for a living and you are the reason I get to do it. I promise to continue to listen, learn, research, test and implement ways to make work better!

About the Authors

Sara Escobar is a workplace strategist and change leader for global companies, including CBRE, Riot Games, Netflix, Hulu, and Honey. She helps organizations solve complex workplace challenges—and believes that improving how we work is the key to improving how we live. She has an MS in Organizational Development from Pepperdine University and lives in Portland, Oregon.

Corinne Murray is a work futurist and workplace strategist helping organizations adapt to the future of work. She has led transformations at WeWork, American Express, RXR, Gensler, and CBRE, with expertise in behavior, hybrid models, and AI's impact on how—and where—we work. She is based on Long Island in New York.

www.ingramcontent.com/pod-product-compliance
Lightning Source LLC
Chambersburg PA
CBHW071546210326
41597CB00019B/3144